The
Complete Book
of
Personal Legal Forms

Daniel Sitarz
Attorney-at-Law

Nova Publishing Company
Legal Publications Division
Boulder, Colorado

Cover design by Christine Jacquot of Spectrum Graphics, Pomona, IL

Manufactured in the United States.

Library of Congress Catalog Card Number 93-086773
ISBN 0-935755-10-1

Library of Congress Cataloging-in-Publication Data
      Sitarz, Dan, 1948-
      The Complete Book of Personal Legal Forms / Daniel Sitarz -- 1st ed.
      248 p. (Legal Self-Help Series) includes index;
      ISBN 0-935755-10-1 : $16.95
      1. Forms (Law)--United States--Popular Works. 2. Civil Law--United States--Forms. I.
      Title. II. Series.
      KF170.S57 1993   346.73'0269   LC93-086773

Nova Publishing Company is dedicated to providing up-to-date and accurate legal information to the public. All Nova publications are periodically revised to contain the latest available legal information.

1st Edition; 1st Printing: November, 1993

This publication is designed to provide accurate and authoritative information in regard to the subject matter covered. It is sold with the understanding that the publisher and author are not engaged in rendering legal, accounting, or other professional services. If legal advice or other expert assistance is required, the services of a competent professional person should be sought.

From a Declaration of Principles jointly adopted by a Committee of the American Bar Association and a Committee of Publishers

DISCLAIMER

NOVA PUBLISHING COMPANY
Legal Publications Division
4882 Kellogg Circle
Boulder CO 80303

Distributed to the trade by:
National Book Network
4720 Boston Way
Lanham MD 20706
1(800)462-6420

TABLE OF CONTENTS

PREFACE

This book is part of Nova Publishing Company's continuing series on Legal Self-Help. The various self-help legal guides in this series are prepared by licensed attorneys who feel that public access to the American legal system is long overdue.

With the proper information, the average person in today's world can easily understand and apply many areas of law. However, historically, there have been concerted efforts on the part of the organized Bar and other lawyer organizations to prevent "self-help" legal information from reaching the general public. These efforts have gone hand-in-hand with an attempt to leave the law cloaked in antiquated and unnecessary legal language; language which, of course, one must pay a lawyer to translate.

Law in American society is far more pervasive than ever before. There are legal consequences to virtually every public and most private actions in today's world. Leaving knowledge of the law within the hands of only the lawyers in such a society is not only foolish, but dangerous as well. A free society depends, in large part, on an informed citizenry. This book and others in Nova's Legal Self-Help series are intended to provide the necessary information to those members of the public who wish to use and understand the law for themselves.

However, in an area as wide-ranging as personal legal forms, encompassing topics as diverse as property law, constitutional law, marital law, wills, trusts, and legal contracts, it is not always prudent to attempt to handle every legal situation which arises without the aid of a competent attorney. Although the information presented in this book will give its readers a basic understanding of the areas of law covered, it is not intended that this text entirely substitute for experienced legal assistance in all situations. Throughout this book there are references to those particular situations in which the aid of a lawyer is strongly recommended.

Regardless of whether or not a lawyer is ultimately retained in certain situations, the legal information in this handbook will enable the reader to understand the framework of law in this country and how to effectively use legal forms in their personal lives.

To try and make that task as easy as possible, technical legal jargon has been eliminated whenever possible and plain English used instead. Naturally, plain and easily-understood English is not only perfectly proper for use in all legal documents but, in most cases, leads to far less confusion on the part of later readers. When it is necessary in this book to use a legal term which may be unfamiliar to most people, the word will be shown in *italics* and defined when first used. A detailed Glossary of legal terms is provided at the end of this book for reference.

CHAPTER 1

USING LEGAL FORMS

American society operates on a daily assortment of legal forms. There are more legal forms in use in America than in any other country on Earth. Individuals are not immune to this flood of legal forms. The legal system in America has a profound impact on everyone. While large corporations are able to hire expensive lawyers to deal with their legal problems and paperwork, most individuals and families can not afford such a course of action. Whether preparing a will, leasing a house, or selling a piece of personal property, individuals must deal with a variety of legal documents throughout their lives, usually without the aid of an attorney.

Unfortunately, many people who are confronted with such forms do not understand the legal ramifications of the use of these forms. They simply sign the lease, or contract, or bill of sale with the expectation that it is a fairly standard document, without any unusual legal provisions. They trust that the details of the particular document will fall within what is considered generally acceptable. In most cases, this may be true. In many situations, however, it is not. Our court system is clogged with cases in which two people are battling over what was really intended by the incomprehensible legal language in a certain contract.

Much of the confusion over legal documents comes from two areas: First, there is a general lack of understanding among most people regarding the framework of contract law. Second, many legal documents are written in antiquated legal jargon that is even difficult for most lawyers to understand and nearly impossible for an average person to comprehend. Although this book will provide an overview of the uses of legal contracts in many standard situations, it is not intended to be a complete reference on the subject of contract law.

The contracts and other various legal documents that are used in this book are, however, written in plain English. Standard legal jargon, as used in most lawyer-prepared documents, is, for most people, totally incomprehensible. Despite the lofty arguments by attorneys regarding the need for such strained and difficult language, the vast majority of legalese is absolutely unnecessary. Clarity, simplicity, and readability should be the goal in legal documents. In most contexts, *buyer* and *seller* or *landlord* and *tenant* or some other straight-forward term of definition of the parties involved is possible.

Unfortunately, certain obscure legal terms are the only words that accurately and precisely describe some things in certain legal contexts. In those few cases, the unfamiliar legal term will be defined when first used. Generally, however, simple terms are used.

All of the legal documents contained in this book have been prepared in essentially the same manner that attorneys use to create legal forms. Many people believe that lawyers prepare each legal document that they compose entirely from scratch. Nothing could be further from the truth. Invariably, lawyers begin their preparation of a legal document with a standardized legal form book. Every law library has multi-volume sets of these encyclopedic texts which contain blank forms for virtually every conceivable legal situation. Armed with these pre-prepared legal forms, lawyers, in many cases, simply fill in the blanks and have their secretaries re-type the form for the client. Of course, the client is generally unaware of this process. As the lawyers begin to specialize in a certain area of legal expertise, they compile their own files containing such blank forms.

This book provides individuals with a set of legal forms which have been prepared with the problems and normal transactions of everyday life in mind. They are intended to be used in those situations that are clearly described by their terms. Of course, while most transactions will fall within the bounds of these normal situations, some legal circumstances will present non-standard situations. The forms in this book are designed to be readily adaptable to most usual situations. They may be carefully altered to conform to the particular transaction that you may be confronted with. However, if you are faced with a complex or tangled legal situation, the advice of a competent lawyer is highly recommended. It may also be advisable to create your legal document for a certain legal situation and have a lawyer check it for any local legal circumstances.

The proper and cautious use of the forms provided in this book will allow the typical person to save considerable money on legal costs. Perhaps more importantly, these forms will provide a method by which the person can avoid costly misunderstandings about what exactly was intended in a particular situation or transaction. By using the forms provided to clearly set out the terms and conditions of everyday personal dealings, disputes over what was really meant can be avoided.

How Use To This Book

In each chapter of this book, you will find an introductory section that will give you an overview of the types of situations in which the forms in that chapter will generally be used. Following that overview, there will be a brief explanation of the specific uses for each form. Included in the information provided for each form will be a discussion of the legal terms and conditions provided in the form. Finally, for each form, there is a listing of the information that must be compiled to complete the form.

The forms in this book may be used in one of two ways. First, photocopies of any form may be made and simply filled in and used as provided. The forms are *not* designed to be torn out. It is expected that the forms may be used on more than one occasion. The preferable manner for using these forms, however, is to make a copy of the form, fill in the information that is necessary, and then re-type the form in its entirety on clean white letter-sized paper. The trend in the legal profession is to move entirely to letter-sized (8 1/2" X 11") paper. In fact, many court systems (including the entire Federal court system) now refuse to accept documents on legal-sized paper.

For purposes of simplification, most of the forms in this book are set out in a form as would be used by two individuals. If businesses are parties to the contract, please identify the name and type of business entity (for example: Jackson Car Stereo, a New York sole proprietorship, etc.) in the first section of the contract. Many of the forms in this book have blanks for inserting the state or county. If you are a resident of Louisiana, substitute *parish* for *county*. If you are a resident of Pennsylvania, Massachusetts, Virginia, or Kentucky, substitute *Commonwealth* for *state*. If you are a resident of Washington D.C., please substitute *District of Columbia* for *state*. In most cases, masculine and feminine terms have been eliminated and the generic *it* or *them* used instead. In the few situations in which this leads to awkward sentence construction, *her/his* or *she/he* may be used instead.

It is recommended that you review the table of contents of this book in order to gain a broad overview of the range and type of legal documents that are available. Then, before you prepare any of the forms for use, you should carefully read the introductory information and instructions in the chapter in which the particular form is contained. Try to be as detailed and specific as possible as you fill in these forms. The more precise the description, the less likelihood that later disputes may develop over what was actually intended by the language chosen.

The careful preparation and use of the legal forms in this book should provide the typical individual with most of the legal documents necessary for day-to-day life. If in doubt as to whether a particular form will work in a specific application, please consult a competent lawyer.

CHAPTER 2

CONTRACTS

The foundation of most agreements is a contract. A *contract* is merely an agreement by which two or more parties each promise to do something. This simple definition of a contract can encompass incredibly complex agreements. The objective of a good contract is to clearly set out the terms of the agreement. Once the parties have reached an oral understanding of what their agreement should be, the terms of the deal should be put in writing. Contrary to what many attorneys may tell you, the written contract should be clearly written and easily understood by both parties to it. It should be written in precise and unambiguous terms. The most common cause for litigation over contracts is arguments over the meaning of the language used. Remember that both sides to the agreement should be able to understand and agree to the language being used.

A contract has to have certain prerequisites to be enforceable in court. These requirements are relatively simple and most will be present in any standard agreement. However, you should understand what the various legal requirements are before you prepare your own contracts. To be enforceable, a contract must have *consideration*. In the context of contract law, this simply means that both parties to the contract must have promised to do something or forego taking some type of action. If one of the parties has not promised to do anything or forego any action, he or she will not be able to legally force the other party to comply with the terms of the contract. There has to be some form of mutual promise for a contract to be valid. For example: A agrees to pay B if B paints a car. A's promise is to pay if the job is completed. B's promise is to paint the car. If B paints the car and is not paid, A's promise to pay can be enforced in court. Similarly, if B fails to paint the car, A can have the contract enforced in court. A and B's mutual promises are the consideration necessary to have a valid and enforceable contract.

Another requirement is that the parties to the contract be clearly identified and the terms of the contract also be clearly spelled out. The terms and description need not be complicated, but they must be in enough detail to enable the parties to the contract (and any subsequent court) to clearly determine what exactly the parties were referring to when they made the contract. In the prior example, the names and addresses of the parties must be included for the contract to be enforceable. In addition, a description of the car must be incorporated in the contract. Finally, a description of the type of paint job and the amount of money to be paid should also be contained in the contract.

The following documents are included for use in situations requiring a basic contract. There are documents for assigning, modifying, extending, and terminating a basic contract. A form for adding exhibits to a contract is also included.

Contract: This basic document can be adapted for use in many situations. The terms of the contract that the parties agree to should be carefully spelled out and inserted where indicated. The other information that is required are the names and addresses of the parties to the contract and the date the contract is to take effect. This basic contract form is set up to accommodate an agreement between two individuals. If a business is party to the contract, please identify the name and type of business entity (for example: Jackson Car Stereo, a New York sole proprietorship, etc.) in the first section of the contract.

Extension of Contract: This document should be used to extend the effective time period during which a contract is in force. The use of this form allows the time limit to be extended without having to entirely re-draft the contract. Under this document, all of the other terms of the contract will remain the same, with only the expiration date changing. You will need to fill in the original expiration date and the new expiration date. Other information necessary will be the names and addresses of the parties to the contract and a description of the contract. A copy of the original contract should be attached to this form.

Modification of Contract: Use this form to modify any other terms of a contract (other than the expiration date). It may be used to change any portion of the contract. Simply note what changes are being made in the appropriate place on this form. If a portion of the contract is being deleted, make note of the deletion. If certain language is being substituted, state the substitution clearly. If additional language is being added, make this clear. A copy of the original contract should be attached to this form. For example, you may wish to use language as follows:

• "Paragraph _____ is deleted from this contract:

• "The following new paragraph is added to this contract:"

Termination of Contract: This document is intended to be used when both parties to a contract mutually desire to end the contract prior to its original expiration date. Under this form, both parties agree to release each other from any claims against each other based on anything in the contract. This document effectively ends any contractual arrangement between two parties. Information necessary to complete this form are the names and addresses of the parties to the contract, a description of the contract, and the effective date of the termination of the contract.

Assignment of Contract: This form is for use if one party to a contract is assigning its full interest in the contract to another party. This effectively substitutes one party for another under a contract. This particular assignment form has both of the parties agreeing to indemnify and hold each other harmless for any failures to perform under the contract while they were the party liable under it. This *indemnify and hold harmless* clause simply means that if a claim arises for failure to perform, each party agrees to be responsible for the period of their own performance obligations. A description of the contract which is assigned should include the parties to the contract, the purpose of the contract, and the date of the contract. Other information that is necessary to complete the assignment is the name and address of the *assignor* (the party who is assigning the contract), the name and address of the *assignee* (the party to whom the contract is being assigned), and the date of the assignment. A copy of the original contract should be attached to this form. A copy of a Consent to Assignment of Contract should also be attached, if necessary.

Consent to Assignment of Contract: This form is used if the original contract states that the consent of one of the parties is necessary for the assignment of the contract to be valid. A description of the contract and the name and signature of the person giving the consent are all that is necessary for completing this form. A copy of the original contract should be attached to this form.

Contract Exhibit: This form may be used with any contract. It provides a simple method for attaching other documents to the contract and having them considered as a legal part of the contract. If you have documents, letters, forms, etc. that you feel are necessary to have as a part of a contract, use this simple form. The space after "Exhibit" in the title of this document is for placing a letter to describe this exhibit (for example: Exhibit A). In the space provided, describe clearly the particular contract which the exhibit is to be attached to (for example: The Contract dated June 1, 1994 between John Smith of 111 Main St., Uptown, NY and Mary Johnson of 222 Broadway Ave., Downtown CA).

CONTRACT

This Contract is made on _____, 19 ___, between _____

_____, residing at _____, City of _____,

State of _____, and _____, residing at _____,

City of _____, State of _____.

For valuable consideration, the parties agree as follows:

1.

2.   No modification of this Contract will be effective unless it is in writing and is signed by both parties. This Contract binds and benefits both parties and any successors. Time is of the essence of this contract. This document, including any attachments, is the entire agreement between the parties. This Contract is governed by the laws of the State of _____.

The parties have signed this Contract on the date specified at the beginning of this Contract.

_____
(Signature)

_____
(Signature)

_____
(Printed name)

_____
(Printed name)

EXTENSION OF CONTRACT

This Extension of Contract is made on _____, 19 ___, between _____, residing at _____, City of _____, State of _____, and _____, residing at _____, City of _____, State of _____.

For valuable consideration, the parties agree as follows:

1.   The following described contract will end on _____, 19 ___:

This contract is attached to this Extension and is a part of this Extension.

2.   The parties agree to extend this contract for an additional period, which will begin immediately on the expiration of the original time period and will end on _____, 19 ___.

3.   The Extension of this contract will be on the same terms and conditions as the original contract. This Extension binds and benefits both parties and any successors. This document, including the attached original contract, is the entire agreement between the parties.

The parties have signed this Extension on the date specified at the beginning of this Extension.

_____   _____
(Signature)   (Signature)

_____   _____
(Printed name)   (Printed name)

MODIFICATION OF CONTRACT

This Modification of Contract is made on _____, 19 ___, between _____, residing at _____, City of_____, State of _____, and _____, residing at _____, City of _____, State of _____.

For valuable consideration, the parties agree as follows:

1. The following described contract is attached to this Modification and is made a part of this Modification:

2. The parties agree to modify this contract as follows:

3. All other terms and conditions of the original contract remain in effect without modification. This Modification binds and benefits both parties and any successors. This document, including the attached contract, is the entire agreement between the parties.

The parties have signed this modification on the date specified at the beginning of this Modification.

_____   _____
(Signature)   (Signature)

_____   _____
(Printed name)   (Printed name)

TERMINATION OF CONTRACT

This Termination of Contract is made on _____, 19 _____, between _____, residing at _____, City of _____, State of _____, and _____, residing at _____, City of _____, State of _____.

For valuable consideration, the parties agree as follows:

1.   The parties are currently bound under the terms of the following described contract, which is attached and is part of this Termination:

2.   They agree to mutually terminate and cancel this contract effective on this date. This Termination Agreement will act as a mutual release of all obligations under this contract for both parties, as if the contract has not been entered into in the first place.

3.   This Termination binds and benefits both parties and any successors. This document, including the attached contract being terminated, is the entire agreement between the parties.

The parties have signed this Termination on the date specified at the beginning of this Termination.

_____   _____
(Signature)   *(Signature)*

_____   _____
(Printed name)   *(Printed name)*

ASSIGNMENT OF CONTRACT

This Assignment is made on _____, 19 ___, between _____
_____, Assignor, residing at _____, City of_____
_____, State of _____, and _____, Assignee,
residing at _____ , City of _____, State of _____.

For valuable consideration, the parties agree to the following terms and conditions:

1.   The Assignor assigns all interest, burdens, and benefits in the following described contract to the Assignee:
This contract is attached to this Assignment and is a part of this Assignment.

2.   The Assignor warrants that this contract is in effect, has not been modified, and is fully assignable. If the consent of a third party is necessary for this Assignment to be effective, such consent is attached to this Assignment and is a part of this Assignment. Assignor agrees to indemnify and hold the Assignee harmless from any claim which may result from the Assignor's failure to perform under this contract prior to the date of this Assignment.

3.   The Assignee agrees to perform all of the obligations of the Assignor and receive all of the benefits of the Assignor under this contract. Assignee agrees to indemnify and hold the Assignor harmless from any claim which may result from the Assignee's failure to perform under this contract after the date of this Assignment.

2.   This Assignment binds and benefits both parties and any successors. This document, including any attachments, is the entire agreement between the parties.

_____   _____
(Signature of Assignor)   *(Signature of Assignee)*

_____   _____
(Printed name of Assignor)   *(Printed name of Assignee)*

CONSENT TO ASSIGNMENT OF CONTRACT

Date: _____

To:

1.   I am a party to the following described contract:

This contract is the subject of the attached Assignment of Contract.

I consent to the Assignment of this Contract as described in the attached Assignment, which provides that the Assignee is substituted for the Assignor.

_____
(Signature)

_____
(Printed name)

CONTRACT EXHIBIT _____

This Contract Exhibit _____ is attached and made part of the following contract:

CHAPTER 3

SIGNATURES AND NOTARY ACKNOWLEDGEMENTS

Signatures and notary acknowledgements for legal forms serve similar but slightly different purposes. Both are used to document the formal signing of a legal instrument, but the notarized acknowledgement also serves as a method of providing a neutral witness to the signature, and so, authenticates the signature. In addition, a notarized acknowledgement can serve an additional purpose of providing a statement under oath. For example, a notarized acknowledgement can be used to assert that a person states, under oath, that he has read the document that he or she is signing and believes that what it contains is the truth.

The use of a notary acknowledgement is not required for all legal forms. The notary acknowledgements contained in this chapter are to be used only for the purpose of providing a notarization required for recording a document. Generally, notarization is only necessary if the document is intended to be recorded with an official government office in some manner. For example, all documents which intend to convey real estate should be recorded in the county recorder's office or register of deeds office in the county (or parish) where the property is located. In virtually all jurisdictions, such documents must be notarized before they will be recorded. Similarly, some states require automobile titles and similar documents to be notarized. Check with your local county clerk to determine the requirements in your locale.

Another unofficial purpose of notarization of legal documents is to make the document seem more important to the parties. By formally having their signatures witnessed by a notary public, they are attesting to the fact that they ascribe a powerful purpose to the document. Although this type of notarization carries with it no legal value, it does serve a valid purpose in solemnizing the signing of an important legal document.

For all of the notary acknowledgement forms contained in this chapter, the following information is necessary:

- The name of the state in which the document is signed,
- The name of the county in which the document is signed;
- The date on which the document is signed;
- The name of the person who is signing the document;
- The name of the notary public (or similar official);
- The state in which the notary is authorized to perform;
- The county in which the notary is registered to act;
- The date on which the notary's commission will expire.

In addition, many states require that the notary place an embossed seal on the document to authenticate the notarization process. The notary who completes the acknowledgement will know the correct procedure for your state.

A simple signature line merely serves to provide a place for a party to a document to sign his or her name. However, care must be taken to be sure that the type of signature line used corresponds exactly with the person or business entity who is joining in the signing of a document.

The following notary acknowledgements and signature lines are intended to be used for the specific purposes outlined below. When preparing a legal document, choose the correct version of these additions carefully. The following are contained in this chapter:

Individual Acknowledgement: This clause should be used on documents where an individual is one of the parties who is to sign the document and the document needs to be notarized. However, if the document is to be signed by a wife and husband together, use the appropriate acknowledgement form which follows.

Individual Signature Line: This line should be inserted on all documents where a party that will sign the document is an individual. Again, however, if the document is to be signed by a wife and husband together, use the appropriate signature line which follows.

Wife and Husband Acknowledgement: This clause should be used on documents where both a wife and husband are to sign the document and the document needs to be notarized.

Wife and Husband Signature Line: This line should be inserted on all documents where both a wife and husband are intended to sign the document.

Power of Attorney Acknowledgement: This clause should be used on documents where an individual acting under a power of attorney is one of the parties who is to sign the document and the document needs to be notarized. As noted in Chapter 4, an *attorney-in-fact* is a person who is authorized to act for another person by virtue of a document entitled a *Power of Attorney*, which will be further explained in the next chapter.

Power of Attorney Signature Line: This line should be inserted on all documents where a party that will sign the document is an individual acting under a power of attorney. The person signing must have the specific authority to act for another person under some form of Power of Attorney. The date of the Power of Attorney form should be noted.

INDIVIDUAL ACKNOWLEDGEMENT

State of _____

County of _____

On _____, 19 ___, _____ personally came before me and, being duly sworn, did state that he/she is the person described in the above document and that he/she signed the above document in my presence.

_____
(Notary signature)

Notary Public, for the County of _____

State of _____

My commission expires: _____

INDIVIDUAL SIGNATURE LINE

_____
(Signature)

_____
(Printed name)

WIFE AND HUSBAND ACKNOWLEDGEMENT

State of _____

County of _____

On _____, 19 __, _____ and _____
personally came before me and, being duly sworn, they did state that they are the wife
and husband described in the above document and that they signed the above document in my presence.

_____
(Notary signature)

Notary Public, for the County of _____

State of _____

My commission expires: _____

WIFE AND HUSBAND SIGNATURE LINE

_____
(Signature)

_____, wife
(Printed name of wife)

_____
(Signature)

_____, husband
(Printed name of husband)

POWER OF ATTORNEY ACKNOWLEDGEMENT

State of _____

County of _____

On _____, 19 ___, _____ personally
came before me and, being duly sworn, did state that he/she is the attorney-in-fact
of _____ described in the above document; that
he/she signed the above document in my presence as attorney-in-fact on behalf of this
person; and that he/she had full authority to do so under Power of Attorney
dated _____, 19 ___.

_____
(Notary signature)

Notary Public, for the County of _____

State of _____

My commission expires: _____

POWER OF ATTORNEY SIGNATURE LINE

_____
(Signature)

_____
(Printed name of person holding power of attorney)

As Attorney-in-fact for _____

Under Power of Attorney dated:_____

CHAPTER 4

POWERS OF ATTORNEY

A *power of attorney* form is a document which is used to allow one person to give authority to another person to act on their behalf. The person signing the power of attorney grants legal authority to another to "stand in their shoes" and act legally for them. The person who receives the power of attorney is called an *attorney-in-fact*. This title and the power of attorney form does not mean that the person receiving the power has to be a lawyer.

Power of attorney forms are useful documents for many occasions. They can be used to authorize someone else to sign certain documents if you can not be present when the signatures are necessary. For example, a real estate closing in another state can be completed without your presence by providing a power of attorney to a real estate agent (or even a friend) which authorizes them to sign the documents on your behalf. Similarly, if you must be away from your home on a trip, and certain actions must be made in your absence, a power of attorney may be granted to enable another person to legally perform on your behalf. They can be used to allow your accountant to negotiate with the IRS or allow your secretary to sign checks and temporarily operate your business, or for many other purposes.

Traditionally, property matters were the type of actions handled with powers of attorney. Increasingly, however, people are using a specific type of power of attorney to authorize other persons to act on their behalf in the event of disability. This broad type of power of attorney is called a *durable* power of attorney. A *durable* power of attorney is intended to remain in effect even if a person becomes disabled or incompetent. All states have passed legislation that specifically authorizes this type of power of attorney. However, a few states require that specific language or forms be used for durable powers of attorney.

(Residents of California, Florida, Missouri, Nevada, New York, North Carolina, Oklahoma, Rhode Island, and South Carolina need to consult with the specific laws in their states to determine any procedures or forms required for durable powers of attorney).

The types of powers of attorney included in this chapter and instructions for their use are as follows:

Unlimited Power of Attorney: This form should be used only in the situation in which you desire to authorize another person to act for you in all transactions. The grant of power under this document is unlimited. However, please be advised that some states may require that you specifically spell out the authority granted to perform certain acts. Generally, however, for personal and property transactions this broad grant of power will be effective. All that is necessary are the names and addresses of the person granting the power and of the person receiving the power. Both persons should sign the document. The signature of the person granting the power should be notarized.

Limited Power of Attorney: This document provides for a limited grant of authority to another person. It should be used if you only need to authorize another to act for you in a specific manner or to perform a specific action. The type of acts that you authorize the other person to perform should be spelled out in detail to avoid confusion. For example: [*to sign any necessary forms to complete the closing of the sale of real estate*]. What is necessary to complete this form are the names and addresses of the person granting the power and of the person receiving the power; and a full and detailed description of the powers granted. Both persons should sign the document. The signature of the person granting the power should be notarized.

Durable Unlimited Power of Attorney: Like the Unlimited Power of Attorney described above, this form should be used only in the situation in which you desire to authorize another person to act for you in all transactions. The grant of power under this document is unlimited. However, unlike the general Unlimited power of attorney, this form remains in effect even if you are incapacitated or disabled. This form also allows your attorney-in-fact to act on your behalf in making medical decisions regarding your care. Please be advised that some states may require that you specifically spell out the authority granted to perform certain acts. Generally, however, for personal and property transactions this broad grant of power will be effective to allow your attorney-in-fact to perform on your behalf in the event of your disability. To complete this form the names and addresses of the person granting the power and of the person receiving the power should be filled in. Both persons should sign the document. The signature of the person granting the power should be notarized.

Durable Limited Power of Attorney: Like the Limited Power of Attorney described above, this document provides for a limited grant of authority to another person. It should be used if you only need to authorize another to act for you in a specific manner or to perform a specific action. However, this form remains in effect even if you are incapacitated or disabled. This form also allows your attorney-in-fact to act on your behalf in making medical decisions regarding your care. Please be advised that some states may require that you specifically spell out the authority granted to perform certain acts. Generally, however, for personal and property transactions the limited grant of power provided by this document will be effective to allow your attorney-in-fact to perform on your behalf in the event of your disability. To complete this form the names and addresses of the person granting the power and of the person receiving the power should be filled in. A full and detailed description of the powers granted should be inserted. Both persons should sign the document. The signature of the person granting the power should be notarized.

Revocation of Power of Attorney: This document may be used with any of the above four power of attorney forms. It is used to terminate the authority that was granted to the other person in the first place. If the grant of power was for a limited purpose, and that purpose is complete, this revocation should be used as soon after the transaction as possible. In any event, if you choose to revoke a power of attorney, a copy of this revocation should be provided to the person to whom the power was given. Copies should also be given to any party that may have had dealings with the attorney-in-fact before the revocation and to any party with whom the attorney-in-fact may be expected to attempt to deal with after the revocation.

UNLIMITED POWER OF ATTORNEY

I, _____, residing at _____, City of _____, State of _____, grant an unlimited power of attorney to _____, residing at _____, City of _____, State of _____, to act as my attorney-in-fact.

I give my attorney-in-fact the maximum power under law to perform any act on my behalf that I could do personally. My attorney-in-fact accepts this appointment and agrees to act in my best interest as he or she considers advisable. This power of attorney may be revoked by me at any time and is automatically revoked on my death.

Dated: _____, 19 _____

_____
(Signature of person granting power of attorney)

State of _____
County of _____

On _____, 19 ___, _____ came before me personally and, under oath, stated that he/she is the person described in the above document and he/she signed the above document in my presence.

_____
(Notary signature)

Notary Public, for the County of _____, State of _____

My commission expires: _____

I accept my appointment as attorney-in-fact.

_____
(Signature of person granted power of attorney)

LIMITED POWER OF ATTORNEY

I, _____, residing at _____, City
of _____, State of _____, grant a limited power of attorney to
_____, residing at _____, City
of _____, State of _____, to act as my attorney-in-fact.

I give my attorney-in-fact the maximum power under law to perform the following
specific acts on my behalf:

My attorney-in-fact accepts this appointment and agrees to act in my best interest as
he or she considers advisable. This power of attorney may be revoked by me at any
time and is automatically revoked on my death.

      Dated: _____, 19 _____

_____
(Signature of person granting power of attorney)

State of _____
County of _____
On _____, 19 ___, _____ came before me
personally and, under oath, stated that he/she is the person described in the above document and he/she signed the above document in my presence.

_____
      (Notary signature)
Notary Public, for the County of _____, State of _____
My commission expires: _____

I accept my appointment as attorney-in-fact.

_____
(Signature of person granted power of attorney)

DURABLE UNLIMITED POWER OF ATTORNEY

I, _____, residing at _____, City

of _____, State of _____, grant an unlimited durable power of

attorney to _____, residing at _____

City of _____, State of _____, to act as my attorney-in-fact.

I give my attorney-in-fact the maximum power under law to perform any acts on my behalf that I could do personally, including the power to make any health decisions on my behalf. My attorney-in-fact accepts this appointment and agrees to act in my best interest as he or she considers advisable. This power of attorney may be revoked by me at any time and is automatically revoked on my death. This power of attorney shall not be affected by my present or future disability or incapacity.

Dated: _____, 19 _____

_____
(Signature of person granting power of attorney)

State of _____

County of _____

On _____, 19 __, _____ came before me personally and, under oath, stated that he/she is the person described in the above document and he/she signed the above document in my presence.

_____
(Notary signature)

Notary Public, for the County of _____, State of _____

My commission expires: _____

I accept my appointment as attorney-in-fact.

_____
(Signature of person granted power of attorney)

DURABLE LIMITED POWER OF ATTORNEY

I, _____, residing at _____, City

of _____, State of _____, grant a limited durable power of attorney

to _____, residing at _____

City of _____, State of _____, to act as my attorney-in-fact.

I give my attorney-in-fact the maximum power under law to perform the following

specific acts on my behalf:

My attorney-in-fact accepts this appointment and agrees to act in my best interest as

he or she considers advisable. This power of attorney may be revoked by me at any

time and is automatically revoked on my death. This power of attorney shall not be af-

fected by my present or future disability or incapacity.

Dated: _____, 19 _____

_____
(Signature of person granting power of attorney)

State of _____

County of _____

On _____, 19 ___, _____ came before me

personally and, under oath, stated that he/she is the person described in the above doc-

ument and he/she signed the above document in my presence.

_____
(Notary signature)

Notary Public, for the County of _____, State of _____

My commission expires: _____

I accept my appointment as attorney-in-fact.

_____
(Signature of person granted power of attorney)

REVOCATION OF POWER OF ATTORNEY

I, _____, residing at _____, City

of _____, State of _____, revoke the Power of Attorney dated

_____, 19 ___, which was granted to _____, residing at

_____, City of _____, State of _____, to

act as my attorney-in-fact.

Dated: _____, 19 _____

_____
(Signature of person revoking power of attorney)

State of _____

County of _____

On _____, 19 ___, _____ came before me

personally and, under oath, stated that he/she is the person described in the above doc-

ument and he/she signed the above document in my presence.

_____
(Notary signature)

Notary Public, for the County of _____, State of _____

My commission expires: _____

CHAPTER 5

WILLS

A *will* is a legal document that, when accepted by a probate court, is proof of an intent to transfer property to the persons or organizations named in the will upon the death of the maker of the will. The maker of the will is known as the *testator*. A will is effective for the transfer of property that is owned by the testator on the date of his death. A will can be changed, modified, or revoked at any time by the testator prior to death.

It is equally important to understand that for a will to be valid, it must generally be prepared, witnessed, and signed according to certain technical legal procedures. Although a will is perfectly valid if it is written in plain English and does not use technical legal language, it **must** be prepared, witnessed, and signed in the manner outlined in this book. This can not be overemphasized. You can not take any shortcuts when following the instructions as they relate to the procedures necessary for completing and signing your will. These procedures are not at all difficult and consist generally of carefully typing your will in the manner outlined later, signing it in the manner specified, and having three witnesses and a notary public also sign the document. (Although not a legal requirement, the notarization of your will can aid in its proof in court later, if necessary). [Note: Wills in this book are not valid for Louisiana residents. Please consult the book: "*Prepare Your Own Will: The National Will Kit*", by Daniel Sitarz (Nova Publishing Company) or contact a competent attorney.]

In some cases (for example, those involving extremely complicated business or personal financial holdings or the desire to create a complex trust arrangement) it is clearly advisable to consult an attorney for the preparation of your will. However, in most circumstances and for most people, the terms of a will which will provide for the necessary protection are relatively routine and may safely be prepared without the added expense of consulting a lawyer.

Before you begin to actually prepare your own will, you must understand what your assets are, who your beneficiaries are to be, and what your personal desires are as to how those assets should be distributed among your beneficiaries. The following Questionnaires will assist you in that task. When you have finished completing these Questionnaires, have them before you as you select and prepare your personal will.

Property Questionnaire Instructions

In general, by the use of a will you may bequeath any property that you own at the time of your death. However, there are forms of property which you may "own", but which may not be transferred by way of a will. In addition, you may own only a percentage or share of certain other property. In such situations, only that share or percentage which you actually own may be left by your will. Finally, there are types of property ownership which are automatically transferred to another party at your death, regardless of the presence of a will.

In the first category of property which can *not* be transferred by will are properties which have a designated beneficiary outside of the provisions of your will. In general, if there is already a valid determination of who will receive the property upon your death (as there is, for example, in the choice of a life insurance beneficiary), you may not alter this choice of beneficiary through the use of your will. If you wish to alter your choice of beneficiary in any of these cases, please directly alter the choice with the holder of the particular property (for instance, the life insurance company or bank). These types of properties include:

- Life insurance policies;
- Retirement plans;
- IRA's and KEOGH's;
- Pension plans;
- Trust bank accounts;
- Living trust assets;
- Payable-on-death bank accounts;
- U.S. Savings Bonds, with payable-on-death beneficiaries.

The next category of property which may have certain restrictions regarding its transfer by will is property in which you may only own a certain share or percentage. Examples of this may be a partnership interest in a company or jointly-held property. Using a will, you may only leave that percentage or fraction of the ownership of the property that is actually yours.

The ownership rights and shares of property owned jointly must be considered. Several states, mostly in the Western United States, follow the *community property* type of marital property system. The community property states are: Arizona, California, Idaho, Louisiana, Nevada, New Mexico, Texas, Washington, and Wisconsin. All property owned by either spouse during a marriage is divided into two types: separate property and community property. *Separate* property consists of all property considered owned entirely by one spouse. Separate property, essentially, is all property owned by the spouse prior to the marriage and kept separate during the marriage; and all property received individually by the spouse by gift or inheritance during the marriage. All other property is considered *community* property. In other words, all property acquired during the marriage by either spouse, unless by gift or inheritance, is community property. Community property is considered to be owned in equal shares by each spouse, regardless of whose efforts actually went into acquiring the property. (One major exception to this general rule is Social Security and Railroad retirement benefits, which are considered to be separate property by Federal law).

Thus, if you are a married resident of a community property state, the property which you may dispose of by will consists of all of your separate property and one-half of your jointly-owned marital community property. The other half of the community property automatically becomes your spouse's sole property on your death. Residents of community property states may also own property jointly as tenant-in-common or as joint tenants.

Residents of all other states are governed by a *common law* property system. Under this system, there is no rule which gives fifty percent ownership of the property acquired during marriage to each spouse. In common law states, the property which you may dispose of with your will consists of all the property held by title in your name, any property which you have earned or purchased with your own money, and any property which you may have been given as a gift or inherited, either before or after your marriage.

If your name alone is on a title document in these states (for instance, a deed or automobile title), then you own it solely. If your name and your spouse's name are both on the document, you generally own it as *tenant's-in-common*, unless it specifically states that your ownership is to be as *joint tenants* or if your state allows for a *tenancy-by-the-entireties* (a form of joint tenancy between married persons). There is an important difference between these types of joint ownership: namely, survivorship. With property owned as tenants-in-common, the percentage or fraction that each tenant-in-common owns is property which may be disposed of under a will. If the property is held as joint tenants or as tenants-by-the entireties, the survivor automatically receives the deceased party's share. Thus, in your will, you may not dispose of any property held in joint tenancy or tenancy-by-the entirety since it already has an automatic legal disposition upon your death.

In common-law states, you may dispose of any property which has your name on the title in whatever share that the title gives you, unless the title is held specifically as joint tenants or tenants-by-the-entireties. You may also dispose of any property which you earned or purchased with your own money, and any property which you have been given as a gift or inherited. If you are married, however, there is a further restriction on your right to dispose of property by will. All common law states protect spouses from total disinheritance by providing a statutory scheme under which a spouse may choose to take a minimum share of the deceased spouse's estate, regardless of what the will states. This effectively prevents any spouse from being entirely disinherited through the use of the common law rules of property (name on the title = ownership of property).

Use the following Questionnaire to determine your assets, liabilities, and net worth.

PROPERTY QUESTIONNAIRE

Assets

Cash And Bank Accounts

(Individual accounts can be left by will; jointly tenancy and payable-on-death accounts can not.)

Checking Account . . . .$ _____
Bank _____
Account # _____
Name(s) on account _____

Savings Account . . . .$ _____
Bank _____
Account # _____
Name(s) on account _____

Certificate of Deposit . . . .$ _____
Held by _____
Expiration date _____
Name(s) on account _____

Other Account . . . .$ _____
Bank _____
Account # _____
Name(s) on account _____

Other Account . . . .$ _____
Bank _____
Account # _____
Name(s) on account _____

Total Cash . . . .$ _____

Life Insurance and Annuity Contracts

(Life insurance benefits can not be left by will.)

Ordinary Life . . . . $ _____
Company _____
Policy # _____
Beneficiary _____
Address _____

Endowment . . . . $ _____

Company _____

Policy # _____

Beneficiary _____

Address _____

Term . . . . $ _____

Company _____

Policy # _____

Beneficiary _____

Address _____

Annuity Contract . . . . $ _____

Company _____

Contract # _____

Beneficiary _____

Address _____

Total Insurance . . . .$ _____

Accounts and Notes Receivable

(Debts payable to you may be left by will.)

Accounts . . . . $ _____

Due from _____

Address _____

Notes . . . . $ _____

Due from _____

Address _____

Other Debts . . . . $ _____

Due from _____

Address _____

Other Debts . . . . $ _____

Due from _____

Address _____

Total Accounts & Notes . . . . $ _____

Stocks

(Ownership of individually-held stock may be left by will.)

Company _____
CUSIP or Certificate # _____
and Type of shares _____
Value . . . . $ _____

Company _____
CUSIP or Certificate # _____
and Type of shares _____
Value . . . . $ _____

Company _____
CUSIP or Certificate # _____
and Type of shares _____
Value . . . . $ _____

Total Stocks . . . . $ _____

Bonds

(Ownership of individually-held bonds may be left by will.)

Company _____
CUSIP or Certificate # _____
and Type of shares _____
Value . . . . $ _____

Company _____
CUSIP or Certificate # _____
and Type of shares _____
Value . . . . $ _____

Company _____
CUSIP or Certificate # _____
and Type of shares _____
Value . . . . $ _____

Total Bonds . . . . $ _____

Business Interests

(Ownership of business interests may generally be left by will.)

Individual Proprietorship
Name _____
Location _____
Type of business _____
Your net value . . . .$ _____

Interest in Partnership
Name _____
Location _____
Type of business _____
Gross value $_____
Percentage Interest _____
Your net value . . . .$ _____

Close Corporation Interest
Name _____
Location _____
Type of business _____
Gross value $_____
Percentage shares held _____
Your net value . . . .$ _____

Total Business Value . . . . $ _____

Real Estate

(Property owned individually or as tenants-in-common may be left by will. Property held in joint tenancy or tenancy-by-entirety may not.)

Personal Residence
Location _____
Value: $ _____
How held and percent held? (Joint Tenants, Tenancy in Common, etc?)
_____/_____%
Value your share . . . . $ _____

Vacation Home
Location _____
Value: $ _____
How held and percent held? (Joint Tenants, Tenancy in Common, etc?)
_____/_____%
Value your share . . . . $ _____

Vacant Land
Location _____
Value: $ _____
How held and percent held? (Joint Tenants, Tenancy in Common, etc?)
_____/_____%
Value your share . . . . $ _____

Income property
Location _____
Value: $ _____
How held and percent held? (Joint Tenants, Tenancy in Common, etc?)
_____/_____%
Value your share . . . . $ _____

Total Real Estate . . . . $ _____

Personal Property

(Personal property owned individually or as a tenant-in-common may be left by will.)

Car . . . . $ _____
Description _____

Boat/other vehicles . . . . $ _____
Description _____

Household furnishings . . . . $ _____
Description _____

Jewelry and furs . . . . $ _____
Description _____

Art work . . . . $ _____
Description _____

Total Personal Property . . . . $ _____

Miscellaneous Assets

Royalties, Patents, Copyrights . . . . $ _____
Description _____

Heirlooms . . . . $ _____
Description _____

Other . . . . $ _____
Description _____

Other . . . . $ _____
Description _____

Total Miscellaneous . . . .$ _____

Employee Benefit and Pension/Profit-sharing Plans

(Retirement benefits can not be left by will.)

Company _____
Plan type _____
Net Value . . . . $ _____

Total Benefit Value . . . . $ _____

Total Assets

(Insert totals from previous pages)

Cash Total . . . . $ _____
Life Insurance Total . . . . $ _____
Accounts & Notes Total . . . .$ _____
Stocks Total . . . . $ _____
Bonds Total . . . . $ _____
Business Total . . . .$ _____
Real Estate Total . . . . $ _____
Personal Property Total . . . . $ _____
Miscellaneous Total . . . . $ _____
Pension Total . . . . $ _____

TOTAL ASSETS . . . . $ _____

Liabilities

Notes and Loans Payable

Payable to _____

Address _____

Term _____ Interest rate _____

Amount Due . . . .$ _____

Payable to _____

Address _____

Term _____ Interest rate _____

Amount Due . . . .$ _____

Total Notes and Loans Payable . . . .$ _____

Accounts Payable

Payable to _____

Address _____

Term _____ Interest rate _____

Amount Due . . . .$ _____

Payable to _____

Address _____

Term _____ Interest rate _____

Amount Due . . . .$ _____

Total Accounts Payable . . . .$ _____

Mortgages Payable

Property location _____

Payable to _____

Address _____

Term _____ Interest rate _____

Amount Due . . . .$ _____

Property location _____

Payable to _____

Address _____

Term _____ Interest rate _____

Amount Due . . . .$ _____

Total Mortgages Payable . . . .$ _____

Taxes Due

Federal Income . . . . $ _____
State Income . . . . $ _____
Personal Property . . . .$ _____
Real Estate . . . . $ _____
Payroll . . . . $ _____
Other . . . .$ _____

Total Taxes Due . . . .$ _____

Credit Card Accounts

Credit Card Account # _____
Credit Card Company _____
Address _____
Amount Due . . . .$ _____

Credit Card Account # _____
Credit Card Company _____
Address _____
Amount Due . . . .$ _____

Total Credit Card Accounts Payable . . . .$ _____

Miscellaneous Liabilities

To Whom Due _____
Address _____
Term _____ Interest rate _____
Amount Due . . . .$ _____

To Whom Due _____
Address _____
Term _____ Interest rate _____
Amount Due . . . .$ _____

To Whom Due _____
Address _____
Term _____ Interest rate _____
Amount Due . . . .$ _____

Total Miscellaneous Liabilities . . . .$ _____

Total Liabilities

(Insert totals from previous pages)

Total Notes and Loans Payable . . . . $ _____
Total Accounts Payable . . . .$ _____
Total Mortgages Payable . . . .$ _____
Total Taxes Due . . . .$ _____
Total Credit Card Accounts . . . . $ _____
Total Miscellaneous Liabilities . . . . $ _____

TOTAL LIABILITIES . . . .$ _____

NET WORTH OF YOUR ESTATE

TOTAL ASSETS . . . .$ _____

minus (-)

TOTAL LIABILITIES . . . .$ _____

equals (=)

YOUR TOTAL NET WORTH . . . .$ _____

Beneficiary Questionnaire Instructions

Any person or organization who receives property under a will is termed a *beneficiary* of that will. Any person or organization may receive property under a will unless they fall into certain narrow categories of disqualification. Those who can receive property as beneficiaries include any family members, the named executor, any illegitimate children (if named specifically), corporations, charities (but see below on possible restrictions) creditors, debtors, and any friends, acquaintances, or even strangers. The few categories of disqualified beneficiaries are as follows:

- An attorney who drafts the will is generally assumed to have used undue influence if he or she is made a beneficiary.

- Many states disqualify any witnesses to the execution of the will. However, to be safe, it is recommended that none of your witnesses be beneficiaries under your will.

- A person who murders a testator is universally disqualified from receiving any property under the murdered person's will.

- An unincorporated association is typically not allowed to receive property under a will. This particular disqualification stems from the fact that such associations generally have no legal right to hold property.

- A few states also have restrictions on the right to leave property to charitable organizations and churches. If you intend to leave large sums of money or property to a charitable organization or church, please check with a competent attorney or consult *"Prepare Your Own Will: The National Will Kit"* by Daniel Sitarz (Nova Publishing Company) for further information on state-by-state restrictions.

You are advised to review your will periodically and make any necessary changes as your marital or family situation may dictate. If you are divorced, married, remarried, or widowed, adopt or have a child, there may be unforeseen consequences based on the way you have written your will. Each state has differing laws on the effect of marriage and divorce on a person's will. Your will should be prepared with regard to how your life is presently arranged. It should, however, always be reviewed and updated each time there is a substantial change in your life.

BENEFICIARY QUESTIONNAIRE

Spouse _____
　　　　Maiden Name _____
　　　　Date of Marriage _____
　　　　Date of Birth _____
　　　　Address _____

　　　　_____
　　　　Current Income $ _____
　　　　Amount, specific items, or share of estate which you desire to leave _____

　　　　_____
　　　　Alternate Beneficiary _____

Child _____
　　　　Date of Birth _____
　　　　Address _____

　　　　_____
　　　　Spouse's Name (if any) _____
　　　　Current Income $ _____
　　　　Amount, specific items, or share of estate which you desire to leave _____

　　　　_____
　　　　Alternate Beneficiary _____

Child _____
　　　　Date of Birth _____
　　　　Address _____

　　　　_____
　　　　Spouse's Name (if any) _____
　　　　Current Income $ _____
　　　　Amount, specific items, or share of estate which you desire to leave _____

　　　　_____
　　　　Alternate Beneficiary _____

Grandchild _____
　　　　Date of Birth _____
　　　　Address _____

　　　　_____
　　　　Spouse's Name (if any) _____
　　　　Current Income $ _____
　　　　Amount, specific items, or share of estate which you desire to leave _____

　　　　_____
　　　　Alternate Beneficiary _____

Grandchild _____

    Date of Birth _____

    Address _____

    _____

    Spouse's Name (if any) _____

    Current Income $ _____

    Amount, specific items, or share of estate which you desire to leave _____

    _____

    Alternate Beneficiary _____

Parent _____

    Date of Birth _____

    Address _____

    _____

    Spouse's Name (if any) _____

    Current Income $ _____

    Amount, specific items, or share of estate which you desire to leave _____

    _____

    Alternate Beneficiary _____

Parent _____

    Date of Birth _____

    Address _____

    _____

    Spouse's Name (if any) _____

    Current Income $ _____

    Amount, specific items, or share of estate which you desire to leave _____

    _____

    Alternate Beneficiary _____

Sibling _____

    Date of Birth _____

    Address _____

    _____

    Spouse's Name (if any) _____

    Current Income $ _____

    Amount, specific items, or share of estate which you desire to leave _____

    _____

    Alternate Beneficiary _____

Sibling _____
      Date of Birth _____
      Address _____

      _____
      Spouse's Name (if any) _____
      Current Income $ _____
      Amount, specific items, or share of estate which you desire to leave _____

      _____
      Alternate Beneficiary _____

Other Dependent _____
      Date of Birth _____
      Address _____

      _____
      Spouse's Name (if any) _____
      Current Income $ _____
      Amount, specific items, or share of estate which you desire to leave _____

      _____
      Alternate Beneficiary _____

Other relatives, friends, or organizations that you wish to leave gifts?

Name _____
      Relationship _____
      Address _____

      _____
      Spouse's Name (if any) _____
      Current Income $ _____
      Amount, specific items, or share of estate which you desire to leave _____

      _____
      Alternate Beneficiary _____

Name _____
      Relationship _____
      Address _____

      _____
      Spouse's Name (if any) _____
      Current Income $ _____
      Amount, specific items, or share of estate which you desire to leave _____

      _____
      Alternate Beneficiary _____

Name _____

    Relationship _____

    Address _____

    _____

    Spouse's Name (if any) _____

    Current Income $ _____

    Amount, specific items, or share of estate which you desire to leave _____

    _____

    Alternate Beneficiary _____

Name _____

    Relationship _____

    Address _____

    _____

    Spouse's Name (if any) _____

    Current Income $ _____

    Amount, specific items, or share of estate which you desire to leave _____

    _____

    Alternate Beneficiary _____

Any persons whom you wish to specifically leave out of your will?

Name _____

    Relationship _____

    Address _____

    _____

    Spouse's Name (if any) _____

    Current Income $ _____

    Reason for disinheritance: _____

    _____

Name _____

    Relationship _____

    Address _____

    _____

    Spouse's Name (if any) _____

    Current Income $ _____

    Reason for disinheritance: _____

    _____

Executor Information List

The following listing will provide your executor with valuable information that will make performance of their difficult task much easier. Included in this questionnaire is information relating to the location of your records, any funeral or burial arrangements that you have made, and lists of important persons which the executor will need to contact after your death. It may be very difficult to confront the need for this information. Please take the time to provide this valuable record of information for your executor. After your death, they may be under tremendous emotional stress and this information will help them perform their necessary duties with the least difficulty. You will probably wish to give this information list and a copy of your will to the person whom you have chosen as your executor.

EXECUTOR INFORMATION LIST

Location of Records

Original of will:
Original of codicil:
Trust documents:
Safe deposit box and key:
Bank book and savings passbook:
Treasury bills and certificates of deposit:
Social Security records:
Real estate deeds and mortgage documents:
Veteran's information:
Stock certificates and bonds:
Promissory notes and loan documents:
Business records:

Partnership records:	
Corporation records:	
Automobile titles:	
Income tax records:	
Credit card records:	
Birth certificate:	
Warranties:	
Other important papers:	

Funeral or Cremation Arrangements

Name of mortuary, funeral service, or crematorium: _____
    Name of person contacted: _____
    Phone #: _____
    Address: _____
    _____
    _____
    Arrangements made:_____
    _____
    _____
    _____
    _____

Name of cemetery: _____
    Name of person contacted: _____
    Phone #: _____
    Address: _____
    _____
    Arrangements made:_____
    _____
    _____
    _____
    _____

Location of memorial or church service: _____

    Name of person contacted: _____

    Phone #: _____

    Address: _____

    _____

    _____

    Arrangements made: _____

    _____

    _____

    _____

    _____

Persons to Contact

Clergy: _____

    Address: _____

    City, State, Zip: _____

    Phone: _____

Lawyer: _____

    Address: _____

    City, State, Zip: _____

    Phone: _____

Accountant: _____

    Address: _____

    City, State, Zip: _____

    Phone: _____

Life Insurance Agent: _____

    Address: _____

    City, State, Zip: _____

    Phone: _____

General Insurance Agent: _____

    Address: _____

    City, State, Zip: _____

    Phone: _____

Employer: _____

    Address: _____

    City, State, Zip: _____

    Phone: _____

Military Unit: _____
    Address: _____
    City, State, Zip: _____
    Phone: _____

Relative name: _____
    Address: _____
    City, State, Zip: _____
    Phone: _____

Relative name: _____
    Address: _____
    City, State, Zip: _____
    Phone: _____

Relative name: _____
    Address: _____
    City, State, Zip: _____
    Phone: _____

Relative name: _____
    Address: _____
    City, State, Zip: _____
    Phone: _____

Friend name: _____
    Address: _____
    City, State, Zip: _____
    Phone: _____

Friend name: _____
    Address: _____
    City, State, Zip: _____
    Phone: _____

Friend name: _____
    Address: _____
    City, State, Zip: _____
    Phone: _____

Preparing and Signing Your Will

Following are three separate wills which have been prepared for certain general situations Please read the description for each will to be certain that the will you chose is appropriate in your particular situation. These will forms are intended to be used as simplified worksheets in preparing your own personal will. They should be filled-in by hand and then re-typed according to the following instructions. These wills are *not* intended to be filled-in and used "as is" as an original will. Such use would most likely result in an invalid will. They *must* be re-typed. Be certain to carefully follow all of the instructions for use of these forms. They are not difficult to fill out, but must be prepared properly to be legally valid. In order to prepare any of the wills in this chapter, you should follow these simple steps:

1. Carefully read through all of the clauses in the blank will to determine if the clauses provided are suitable in your situation. Choose the will that is most appropriate. Make a photo-copy of the will that you choose to use as a worksheet. If you wish, you may use this book itself as a worksheet (unless it is a library book!)

2. Using your Property and Beneficiary Questionnaires, fill in the appropriate information where necessary on these forms. As you fill in the information for each clause, keep in mind the following instructions:

>   **Title Clause:** The title clause is *mandatory* for all wills and must be included. Fill in the name blank with your full legal name. If you have been known under more than one name, use your principal name.

>   **Identification Clause:** The identification clause is *mandatory* and must be included in all wills. In the first blank, include any other names which you are known by. Do this by adding the phrase: "also known as" after your principal full name. For example: *John James Smith, also known as Jimmy John Smith.* In the spaces provided for your residence, use the location of your principal residence; where you currently live permanently.

>   **Marital Status Clause:** Each of the wills in this chapter are for a specific marital status situation. Select the proper will and fill in the appropriate information in this clause.

>   **Identification of Children Clause:** This clause will only be present in the will which relates to children. In this clause, you should specifically identify all of your children, indicating their names, current addresses, and dates of birth. Cross out those spaces which are not used.

Identification of Grandchildren Clause: This clause will only be used in the will which relates to children. If you do not have grandchildren, cross out this entire clause. If you do have grandchildren, in this clause you should specifically identify all of your grandchildren, indicating their names, current addresses, and dates of birth. Cross out those spaces which are not used.

Specific Gifts Clause: For making specific gifts, use as many of the "I give . . ." paragraphs as is necessary to complete your chosen gifts. In these paragraphs, you may make any type of gift that you wish, either a cash gift, a gift of a specific piece of personal property or real estate, or a specific share of your total estate. If you wish to give some of your estate in the form of portions of the total, it is recommended to use fractional portions. Always describe the property in as detailed and clear a manner as possible. Although none of the wills in this chapter contain a specific clause which states that you give one person your entire estate, you may make such a gift using this clause by simply stating: "I give my entire estate to ...". Be sure that you do not then attempt to give any other gifts. However, you should still include the Residuary clause in your will, which is explained below.

A few type of gifts are possible but are not addressed in the wills that may be prepared using this book. Simple shared gifts (for example: I give all my property to my children, Alice, Bill, and Carl, in equal shares) are possible using this book. However, any complex shared gift arrangements will require the assistance of an attorney. In addition, you may impose simple conditions on any gifts in wills prepared using this book. However, complex conditional gifts which impose detailed requirements that the beneficiary must comply with in order to receive the gift are also beyond the scope of this book. Finally, although it is possible to leave any gifts under your will in many types of trusts, a simple trust for leaving gifts to children is the only trust available for wills prepared using this book. If you desire to leave property in trust to an adult through the use of a will, you are advised to seek competent legal advice.

Always describe the beneficiaries in as precise and clear a manner as is possible and by use of their full name. You can also name joint beneficiaries, such as several children, if you choose. The space provided for an identification of the relationship of the beneficiary can be simply a descriptive phrase like "my wife", or "my brother-in-law", or "my best friend". It does not mean that the beneficiary must be related to you personally.

The choice of alternate beneficiary is for the purpose of allowing you to designate someone to receive the gift if your first choice to receive the gift dies before you do (or, in the case of a organization chosen as primary beneficiary, is no longer in business). Your choice for alternate beneficiary may be one or more persons or an organization. You may delete the alternate beneficiary choice and substitute the words "the residue" instead. The result of this change will be that if your primary beneficiary dies before you do, your intended gift to that beneficiary will pass under your Residuary clause, which is discussed below. If additional gifts are desired, simply photo-copy an additional page.

Residuary Clause: Although not a technical legal requirement, a residuary clause is included in every will in this book. With it, you will choose the person, persons, or organization to receive anything not covered by other clauses of your will. Even if you feel that you have given away everything that you own under other clauses of your will, this can be a very important clause. If, for any reason, any other gifts under your will are not able to completed, this clause goes into effect. If there is no residuary clause included in your will, any property not disposed of under your will is treated as though you did not have a will and could potentially be forfeited to the state.

In addition, you may use this clause to give all of your estate (*except* your specific gifts) to one or more persons. For example: you make specific gifts of $1,000 to a sister and a car to a friend. By then naming your spouse as the residuary clause beneficiary, you will have gifted everything in your estate to your spouse--*except* the $1,000 and the car. You could then name your children, in equal shares, as the alternate residuary beneficiaries. In this manner, if your spouse were to die first, your children would then equally share your entire estate--*except* the $1,000 and the car.

Survivorship Clause: This clause is included in each will. This clause provides for two possibilities. First, it provides for a required period of survival for any beneficiary to receive a gift under your will. The second portion of this clause provides for a determination of how your property should pass in the eventuality that both you and a beneficiary (most likely your spouse) should die in a manner that makes it impossible to determine who died first.

If you and your spouse are both preparing wills, it is a good idea to be certain that each of your wills contains identical survivorship clauses. If you are each others primary beneficiary, it is also wise to attempt to coordinate who your alternate beneficiaries may be in the event of a simultaneous death.

Executor Clause: The executor clause is included in every will. With this clause, you will make your choice of *executor*, the person who will administer and distribute your estate and an alternate choice if your first choice is unable to serve. A spouse, sibling, or other trusted party is usually chosen to act as executor. The person chosen should be a resident of the state in which you currently reside.

Be sure to clearly identify the executor and alternate executor by full name. The space provided for an identification of the relationship of the executor can be simply a descriptive phrase like "my wife", or "my brother-in-law", or "my best friend". It does not mean that the executor must be related to you personally.

Child Guardianship Clause: This clause will only be present in the will which relates to children. With this clause you may designate your choice as to whom you wish to care for any of your minor children after you are gone. If you are married, your present spouse is generally appointed by the probate or family court, regardless of your designation in a will. However, even if you are married, it is a good idea to choose your spouse as first choice and then provide a second choice. This will cover the contingency in which both you and your spouse die in a single accident.

Your choice should obviously be a trusted person whom you feel would provide the best care for your children in your absence. Be aware, however, that the court is guided, but not bound, by this particular choice in your will. The court's decision in appointing a child's guardian is based upon what would be in the best interests of the child. In most situations, however, a parent's choice as to who should be their child's guardian is almost universally followed by the courts. Additionally, you grant the guardian broad power to care for and manage your children's property and also provide that the appointed guardian not be required to post a bond in order to be appointed.

Be sure to clearly identify the guardian and alternate guardian by full name. The space provided for an identification of the relationship of the guardian can be simply a descriptive phrase like "my wife", or "my brother-in-law", or "my best friend". It does not mean that the guardian must be related to you personally.

Children's Trust Fund Clause: This clause is only present in the will which relates to children. It is with this clause that you may set up a Trust Fund for any gifts you have made to your minor children. You also may delay the time when they will actually have unrestricted control over your gift. It is not recommended, however, to attempt to delay receipt of control beyond the age of 30. If you have left assets to more than one child, this clause provides that individual trusts be set up for each child.

The choice for trustee under a children's trust should generally be the same person as you have chosen to be the children's guardian. This is not, however, a requirement. The choice of trustee is generally a spouse if alive, with the alternate being a trusted friend or family member. Be sure to clearly identify the trustee and alternate trustee by full name. The space provided for an identification of the relationship of the trustee can be simply a descriptive phrase like "my wife", or "my brother-in-law", or "my best friend". It does not mean that the trustee must be related to you personally.

Signature Clause: The signature lines and final paragraph of your will are mandatory and must be included in your will. You will fill in the number of pages and the appropriate dates where indicated after you have properly typed or had your will typed.

3. After you have filled in all of the appropriate information, carefully re-read your entire will. Be certain that it contains all of the correct information that you desire. Then starting at the beginning of the will, cross out all of the words and phrases in the will that do not apply in your situation.

4. For any of these wills, a Self-Proving Affidavit should also be prepared. Please consult the information and form for the Affidavit that is provided at the end of this chapter.

5. Type your entire will and the Self-Proving Affidavit on clean white sheets of 8 1/2" X 11" paper. Make sure that there are no corrections or erasures on the final copy. If you make a mistake, re-type that particular page. Do not attempt to correct the mistakes on the final copy. After you have successfully had your will typed in the proper form, you are ready to sign it. *Do not* sign your will until you have all of the necessary witnesses and Notary Public present. Select 3 (three) witnesses who will be available to assist you in witnessing your will. These persons may be any adults who are not mentioned in the will either as a beneficiary, executor, trustee, or guardian. They may be friends, neighbors, co-workers, even strangers. However, it is prudent to choose persons who have been stable members of your community, since they may be called upon to testify in court someday. Arrange for all of your witnesses to meet you at the office or home of a local Notary Public. Many banks, real estate offices, and government offices have notary services and most will be glad to assist you. (The Notary Public may *not* be one of the required three witnesses.)

6. In front of all of the witnesses and in front of the Notary Public, the following should take place in the order shown:

You should state: "This is my Last Will and Testament, which I am about to sign. I ask that each of you witness my signature." There is no requirement that the witnesses know any of the terms of your will or that they read any of your will. All that is necessary is that they hear you state that it is your will, that you request them to be witnesses, that they observe you sign your will and that they also sign the will as witnesses in each other's presence.

You will then sign your will at the end, exactly as your name is typewritten on your will, in the two (2) places indicated, in ink using a pen. Don't forget that one of your signatures will be on the "Self-Proving Affidavit".

After you have signed, pass your will to the first witness, who should sign in the two (2) places indicated and fill in his or her address. Don't forget that one of the two places that each witness will sign is on the "Self-Proving Affidavit".

After the first witness has signed, have the will passed to the second Witness, who should also sign in the two (2) places indicated and fill in his or her address.

After the second witness has signed, have the will passed to the third and final witness, who also signs in the two (2) places indicated and fills in his or her address. Throughout this ceremony, you and all of the witnesses must remain together. It is easier if you are all seated around a table or desk.

The final step is for the Notary Public to sign the Self-Proving Affidavit in the space indicated. When this step is completed, your will is a valid legal document and you may be assured that your wishes will be carried out upon its presentation to a probate court on your death.

Please note that you should *never* under any circumstances sign a duplicate of your will. Once it has been properly executed following the steps above, you may make photocopies of your will. It is a good idea to label any of these as "COPIES".

A final precaution is, if you desire, to allow the executor whom you have named to keep a copy of your will. Be careful, however, to be certain that you immediately inform him or her of any new wills which you prepare or of any *codicils* to your will (formal changes to your will) or of any decision to revoke your will. For instructions and a codicil for changing your will, please see section on *Codicils* at the end of this chapter.

Will for Married Person with Children (using Children's Trust)

This will is appropriate for use by a married person with one or more minor children, who desires to place the property and assets which may be left to the children in a trust fund. In addition, this will allows the parent to chooses a person to act as guardian for the child or children. In most cases, a married person may desire to chose the other spouse as both trustee and guardian for any of their children, although this is not a legal requirement. Each spouse/parent must prepare their own will. *Do not* attempt to prepare a joint will for both of you together.

This will contains the following standard clauses:

- Title Clause
- Identification Clause
- Marital Status Clauses
- Children Identification Clause
- Grandchildren Identification Clause
- Specific Gifts Clause
- Residuary Clause
- Survivorship Clause
- Executor Clause
- Guardianship Clause
- Children's Trust Fund Clause
- Signature and Witness Clause

Fill in each of the appropriate blanks in this will using the information which you included in your Property and Beneficiary Questionnaires. Cross out any information that is not appropriate to your situation and re-type the entire will on clean white letter-sized paper.

LAST WILL AND TESTAMENT OF _____

I, _____, residing at
_____, City of _____, State of _____
_____, declare that this is my Last Will and Testament and I revoke all
previous wills and codicils.

I am married to _____.

I was previously married to _____.
That marriage ended on _____, 19 _____,
by _____.

I have _____children living. Their names, addresses, and
dates of birth are as follows:

I have _____ grandchildren living. Their names,
addresses, and dates of birth are as follows:

I make the following specific gifts:

I give _____
_____
to _____,
who is my _____, or if not surviving
to_____,
who is my _____.

I give _____

_____

to _____,

who is my _____, or if not surviving

to_____,

who is my _____.

I give _____

_____

to _____,

who is my _____, or if not surviving

to_____,

who is my _____.

I give _____

_____

to _____,

who is my _____, or if not surviving

to_____,

who is my _____.

I give all the rest of my property, whether real or personal, wherever located, to

_____, who is my

_____, or if not surviving

to_____, who is my

_____.

All beneficiaries named in this will must survive me by thirty days to receive any gift under this will. If any beneficiary and I should die simultaneously, I shall be conclusively presumed to have survived that beneficiary for purposes of this will.

I appoint _____, who is my _____
residing at _____, City of _____, State of _____, as Executor, to serve without bond. If not surviving or otherwise unable to serve, I appoint _____ , who is my _____, residing at _____, City of_____, State of _____, as Alternate Executor, also to serve without bond.

In addition to any powers, authority, and discretion granted by law, I grant such Executor or Alternate Executor any and all powers to perform any acts, in his or her sole discretion and without court approval, for the management and distribution of my estate, including independent administration of my estate.

If a Guardian is needed for any of my minor children, I appoint _____
_____, who is my _____, residing at _____, City of_____, State of _____ as Guardian of the person(s) and property of my minor children, to serve without bond. If not surviving or unable to serve, I appoint _____, who is my _____
_____, residing at _____, City of _____, State of _____ as alternate Guardian, also to serve without bond.

In addition to any powers, authority, and discretion granted by law, I grant such Guardian or Alternate Guardian any and all powers to perform any acts, in his or her sole discretion and without court approval, for the management and distribution of the property of my minor children.

If any of my children are under _____ years of age on my death, I direct that any property that I give them under this will be held in an individual trust for each child, under the following terms, until each shall reach _____ years of age.

    A. I appoint _____, who is my _____,
    residing at _____, City of _____, State of _____, as
    trustee of any and all required trusts, to serve without bond. If not surviving or
    otherwise unable to serve, then I appoint _____,

_____, who is my _____,
residing at _____, City of _____, State of ____,
as alternate Trustee, also to serve without bond. In addition to all powers, authority, and discretion granted by law, I grant such trustee or alternate trustee full power to perform any act, in his or her sole discretion and without court approval, to distribute and manage the assets of any such trust.

B. In the trustee's sole discretion, the trustee may distribute any or all of the principal, income, or both as deemed necessary for the beneficiary's health, support, welfare, and education. Any income not distributed shall be added to the trust principal.

C. Any such trust shall terminate when the beneficiary reaches the required age, when the beneficiary dies prior to reaching the required age, or when all trust funds have been distributed. Upon termination, any remaining undistributed principal and income shall pass to the beneficiary; or if not surviving, to the beneficiary's heirs; or if none, to the residue of my estate.

I publish and sign this Last Will and Testament, consisting of _____ typewritten pages, on _____, 19 _____, and declare that I do so freely, for the purposes expressed, under no constraint or undue influence, and that I am of sound mind and of legal age.

_____
(Signature of Testator)

_____
(Printed name of Testator)

On _____, 19 _____, in the presence of all of us, the above-named Testator published and signed this Last Will and Testament, and then at Testator's request, and in Testator's presence, and in each other's presence, we all signed below as witnesses, and we declare, under penalty of perjury, that, to the best of our knowledge, the Testator signed this instrument freely, under no constraint or undue influence, and is of sound mind and legal age.

_____
(Signature of Witness)

_____
(Printed name of Witness)

_____
(Address of Witness)

_____
(Signature of Witness)

_____
(Printed name of Witness)

_____
(Address of Witness)

_____
(Signature of Witness)

_____
(Printed name of Witness)

_____
(Address of Witness)

Will for Married Person with No Children

This will is appropriate for use by a married person with no children or grandchildren. It allows for a married person to make specific gifts of property to any persons or organizations that they have chosen and to choose an executor.

This will contains the following standard clauses:

- Title Clause
- Identification Clause
- Marital Status Clauses
- Specific Gifts Clause
- Residuary Clause
- Survivorship Clause
- Executor Clause
- Signature and Witness Clause

Fill in each of the appropriate blanks in this will using the information which you included in your Property and Beneficiary Questionnaires. Cross out any information that you do not use and re-type this entire document.

LAST WILL AND TESTAMENT OF _____

I, _____, residing at
_____, City of _____, State of ____
_____, declare that this is my Last Will and Testament and I revoke all
previous wills and codicils.

I am married to _____.

I was previously married to _____.
That marriage ended on _____, 19 _____,
by   _____.

I have no children or grandchildren living.

I make the following specific gifts:

I give _____
_____
to _____,
who is my _____, or if not surviving
to_____,
who is my _____.

I give _____
_____
to _____,
who is my _____, or if not surviving
to_____,
who is my _____.

I give _____

_____

to _____,

who is my _____, or if not surviving

to_____,

who is my _____.

I give _____

_____

to _____,

who is my _____, or if not surviving

to_____,

who is my _____.

I give all the rest of my property, whether real or personal, wherever located, to

_____, who is my

_____, or if not

surviving to_____, who is my

_____.

All beneficiaries named in this will must survive me by thirty days to receive any gift under this will. If any beneficiary and I should die simultaneously, I shall be conclusively presumed to have survived that beneficiary for purposes of this will.

I appoint _____, who is my _____

residing at _____, City of _____, State of _____, as Executor, to serve without bond. If not surviving or otherwise unable to serve, I appoint

_____ , who is my _____,

residing at _____, City of_____, State of _____, as Alternate Executor, also to serve without bond.

In addition to any powers, authority, and discretion granted by law, I grant such Executor or Alternate Executor any and all powers to perform any acts, in his or her sole discretion and without court approval, for the management and distribution of my estate, including independent administration of my estate.

I publish and sign this Last Will and Testament, consisting of _____ typewritten pages, on _____, 19 _____, and declare that I do so freely, for the purposes expressed, under no constraint or undue influence, and that I am of sound mind and of legal age.

_____
(Signature of Testator)

_____
(Printed name of Testator)

On _____, 19 _____, in the presence of all of us, the above-named Testator published and signed this Last Will and Testament, and then at Testator's request, and in Testator's presence, and in each other's presence, we all signed below as witnesses, and we declare, under penalty of perjury, that, to the best of our knowledge, the Testator signed this instrument freely, under no constraint or undue influence, and is of sound mind and legal age.

_____
(Signature of Witness)

_____
(Printed name of Witness)

_____
(Address of Witness)

_____
(Signature of Witness)

_____
(Printed name of Witness)

_____
(Address of Witness)

_____
(Signature of Witness)

_____
(Printed name of Witness)

_____
(Address of Witness)

Will for Single Person with No Children

This will is appropriate for use by a single person with no children or grandchildren. It allows for a single person to make specific gifts of property to any persons or organizations that they have chosen and to choose an executor. It should only be used by a single person who has never been previously married.

This will contains the following standard clauses:

- Title Clause
- Identification Clause
- Marital Status Clauses
- Specific Gifts Clause
- Residuary Clause
- Survivorship Clause
- Executor Clause
- Signature and Witness Clause

Fill in each of the appropriate blanks in this will using the information which you included in your Property and Beneficiary Questionnaires. Cross out any information that you do not use and re-type this entire document.

LAST WILL AND TESTAMENT OF _____

I, _____, residing at

_____, City of _____, State of _____

_____, declare that this is my Last Will and Testament and I revoke all

previous wills and codicils.

I have never been married and I have no children or grandchildren.

I make the following specific gifts:

I give _____

_____

to _____,

who is my _____, or if not surviving

to_____,

who is my _____.

I give _____

_____

to _____,

who is my _____, or if not surviving

to_____,

who is my _____.

I give all the rest of my property, whether real or personal, wherever located, to

_____, who is my

_____, or if not

surviving to_____, who is my

_____.

All beneficiaries named in this will must survive me by thirty days to receive any gift under this will. If any beneficiary and I should die simultaneously, I shall be conclusively presumed to have survived that beneficiary for purposes of this will.

I appoint _____, who is my _____ residing at _____, City of _____, State of _____, as Executor, to serve without bond. If not surviving or otherwise unable to serve, I appoint _____ , who is my _____, residing at _____, City of_____, State of _____, as Alternate Executor, also to serve without bond.

In addition to any powers, authority, and discretion granted by law, I grant such Executor or Alternate Executor any and all powers to perform any acts, in his or her sole discretion and without court approval, for the management and distribution of my estate, including independent administration of my estate.

I publish and sign this Last Will and Testament, consisting of _____ typewritten pages, on _____, 19 _____, and declare that I do so freely, for the purposes expressed, under no constraint or undue influence, and that I am of sound mind and of legal age.

_____
(Signature of Testator)

_____
(Printed name of Testator)

On _____, 19 _____, in the presence of all of us, the above-named Testator published and signed this Last Will and Testament, and then at Testator's request, and in Testator's presence, and in each other's presence, we all signed below as witnesses, and we declare, under penalty of perjury, that, to the best of our knowledge, the Testator signed this instrument freely, under no constraint or undue influence, and is of sound mind and legal age.

_____
(Signature of Witness)

_____
(Printed name of Witness)

_____
(Address of Witness)

_____
(Signature of Witness)

_____
(Printed name of Witness)

_____
(Address of Witness)

_____
(Signature of Witness)

_____
(Printed name of Witness)

_____
(Address of Witness)

Self-Proving Affidavit

Although use of this clause is not a strict legal necessity, it is strongly recommended that you prepare and use this Affidavit with all wills. Although a few states have not enacted legislation to allow for their use in court, the current trend is for all courts to allow their use. This Affidavit will allow for your signature on your will to be proved without the necessity of having the three witnesses appear in court, a point which will save time, money, and trouble in having your will admitted to probate when necessary.

Prepare this document as you have prepared your will. It should then be signed by you (the testator) and your witnesses in front of a notary public. The notary public should then sign the document where indicated.

SELF-PROVING AFFIDAVIT

We, the undersigned Testator and witnesses, being first sworn on oath and under penalty of perjury, state that, in the presence of all the witnesses, the Testator published and signed the above Last Will and Testament and then, at Testator's request, and in the presence of the Testator and of each other, each of the witnesses signed as witnesses, and that, to the best of our knowledge, the Testator signed said Last Will and Testament freely, under no constraint or undue influence, and is of sound mind and legal age.

_____
(Signature of Testator)

_____
(Printed name of Testator)

_____
(Signature of Witness)

_____
(Printed name of Witness)

_____
(Address of Witness)

_____
(Signature of Witness)

_____
(Printed name of Witness)

_____
(Address of Witness)

_____

(Signature of Witness)

_____

(Printed name of Witness)

_____

(Address of Witness)

County of _____} SS.

State of _____}

Subscribed, sworn to, and acknowledged before me on _____, 19____

by _____, the Testator, and

by _____,

_____,

_____,

the Witnesses.

_____

(Signature of Notary Public)

Notary Public, In and for the County of _____,

State of _____.

Changing Your Will

It is most important to follow these instructions carefully should you desire to make **any** changes to your will. Failure to follow these instructions and an attempt to change your will by such methods as crossing out a name or penciling in an addition could have the disastrous effect of voiding portions of or, perhaps, even your entire will. Again, these instructions are not difficult to follow, but are very important to insure that your will remains legally valid. If you desire to totally revoke your will, there are two acceptable methods:

- By signing a new will which expressly states that you revoke all prior wills. All wills prepared using this book contain such a provision.

- By completely destroying, burning, or mutilating your will, while it is in your possession if you actually intend that there be a revocation of your will.

There are also two methods for changing your will. Although it is possible to completely re-write your will to take account of any changes, an easier method is to prepare and formally execute a *codicil*, or a written change to a will. Please bear in mind that all of the formalities surrounding the signing of your original will must again be followed for any such changes contained in a codicil to your will to be valid.

Never attempt to change any portions of your will by any other method. For example, *do not* attempt to add provisions in the margin of your will, either by typing them in or by writing them in. *Do not* attempt to cross-out any portions of your will. These methods are not acceptable methods for the alteration of a will, and could subject your will to a court battle to determine its subsequent validity.

The following is a general form for a codicil and standard clauses for changing provisions of your will. Insert such changes as are necessary where indicated on the form. Prepare it as you prepared your original will using the following simple list of instructions:

1. Make a photo-copy of the codicil. Using the photo-copy as a worksheet, fill in the appropriate information on each chosen clause. On your photo-copy worksheet version, cross out all of the instructions and any other extraneous material which will not be a part of your final codicil. Carefully re-read your entire codicil to be certain that it is exactly as you wish.

2. After making any necessary changes, type or have typed the entire codicil on good quality 8 1/2 X 11" typing paper. Type the "Self-Proving Affidavit" on a separate sheet of paper, as it is technically not a part of your codicil, but rather a separate and distinct document. After you have completed typing your codicil, fill

in the total number of pages in the Signature paragraph. Do not yet sign your codicil or fill in the date in any of the spaces indicated.

3. Again, very carefully proofread your entire codicil. Be certain that there are no errors. If there are any errors, re-type that particular page. *Do not* attempt to correct any errors with white-out type correcting fluid or with erasures of any kind. *Do not* cross-out or add anything to the typewritten words using a pen or pencil. When you have a perfect original of your codicil, with no corrections and no additions, staple all of the pages together in the top left hand corner. The Self-Proving Affidavit should be stapled together at the end of your codicil also. You are now ready to prepare for the *execution* (signing) of your codicil and the Affidavit. For signing your codicil and Affidavit, please follow the same instructions that are provided in earlier in this chapter for signing your will.

CODICIL TO THE LAST WILL AND TESTAMENT OF

_____

I, _____, residing at

_____, City of _____, State of ____,

make this Codicil to my Last Will and Testament dated _____, 19 ___.

I add the following paragraph to my will:

I revoke that portion of my will that reads as follows:

I change the _____ paragraph of my will to read as follows:

I republish my Last Will and Testament, dated _____, 19 _____, as modified
by this Codicil. I have signed this Codicil to my Will, consisting of _____
_____ typewritten pages, on _____, 19 _____, and declare
that I do so freely, for the purposes expressed, under no constraint or undue influence,
and that I am of sound mind and of legal age.

_____
(Signature of Testator)

_____
(Printed name of Testator)

On _____, 19 _____, in the presence of all of us, the above-named Testator published and signed this Codicil to Last Will and Testament, and then at Testator's request, and in Testator's presence, and in each other's presence, we all signed below as witnesses, and we declare, under penalty of perjury, that, to the best of our knowledge, the Testator signed this instrument freely, under no constraint or undue influence, and is of sound mind and legal age.

_____
(Signature of Witness)

_____
(Printed name of Witness)

_____
(Address of Witness)

_____
(Signature of Witness)

_____
(Printed name of Witness)

_____
(Address of Witness)

_____
(Signature of Witness)

_____
(Printed name of Witness)

_____
(Address of Witness)

CHAPTER 6

LIVING WILL

A *living will* is a relatively new legal document which has been made necessary by the advent of recent technological advances in the field of medicine which can allow for the continued existence of a person on advanced life support systems long after any normal semblance of "life", as many people consider it, has ceased. The inherent problem which is raised by this type of extraordinary medical "life support" is that the person whose life is being artificially continued by such means may not wish to be kept alive beyond what they may consider to be the proper time for their life to end. However, since a person in such condition has no method of communicating their wishes to the medical or legal authorities in charge, a living will was developed which allows one to make these important decisions in advance of the situation.

As more and more advances are made in the medical field in terms of the ability to prevent "clinical" death, the difficult situations envisioned by a living will are destined to occur more often. The legal acceptance of a living will is currently at the forefront of new laws being added in many states.

Although this living will does not address all possible contingencies regarding terminally ill patients, it does provide a written declaration for the individual to make known his or her decisions on life-prolonging procedures. A living will declares your wishes not to be kept alive by artificial or mechanical means if you are suffering from a terminal condition and your death would be imminent without the use of such artificial means. It provides a legally-binding written set of instructions regarding your wishes about this important matter.

In order to qualify for the use of a living will, you must meet the following criteria:

- You must be at least 19 years of age;

- You must be of "sound mind" and able to comprehend the nature of your action in signing such a document.

If you desire that your life not be prolonged artificially when there is no reasonable chance for recovery and death is imminent, please follow the instructions below for completion of your living will. The entire following form is mandatory. It has been adapted to be valid in all states which currently recognize living wills. Even in those states that have not yet enacted legislation providing express statutory recognition of living wills, courts, health care professionals, and physicians will be guided by this expression of your desires concerning life support.

Preparing and Signing a Living Will

1. Make a photo-copy of the entire living will form from this chapter. Using the photo-copy as a worksheet, please fill in the correct information in the appropriate blanks. On clean, white, 8 1/2 X 11" paper, have typed or type yourself the entire living will exactly as shown with your information added. Carefully re-read this original living will to be certain that it exactly expresses your desires on this very important matter. When you have a clean, clear original typed version, staple all of the pages together in the upper left-hand corner. *Do not* yet sign this document or fill in the date.

2. You should now assemble three witnesses and a Notary Public to witness your signature. As noted on the document itself, these witnesses should have no connection with you from a health care or beneficiary standpoint. Specifically, the witnesses must:

- Be at least 19 years of age.

- Not be related to you in any manner: by blood, marriage, or adoption.

- Not be your attending physician, or a patient or employee of your attending physician; or a patient, physician, or employee of the health care facility in which you may be a patient. However, please see below.

- Not be entitled to any portion of your estate on your death under any laws of intestate succession, nor under your will or any codicil.

- Have no claim against any portion of your estate on your death.

- Not be directly financially responsible for your medical care.

- Not have signed the living will *for* you, even at your direction.

- Not be paid a fee for acting as a witness.

- In addition, please note that several states and the District of Columbia have laws in effect regarding witnesses when the declarant is a patient in a nursing home, boarding facility, hospital, or skilled or intermediate health care facility. In those situation, it is advisable to have a patient ombudsman, patient advocate, or the director of the health care facility to act as the third witness to the signing of a living will.

4. In front of all of the witnesses and in front of the Notary Public, the following should take place in the order shown:

- You should state: "This is my Living Will which I am about to sign. I ask that each of you witness my signature." There is no requirement that the witnesses know any of the terms of your living will or that they read any of your living will. All that is necessary is that they hear you state that it is your living will, that you request them to be witnesses, that they observe you sign your living will and that they also sign the living will as witnesses in each other's presence.

- You will then sign your living will at the end, exactly as your name is typewritten on your living will, where indicated, in ink using a pen. After you have signed, pass your living will to the first witness, who should sign where indicated and fill in his or her address.

- After the first witness has signed, have the living will passed to the second witness, who should also sign where indicated. After the second witness has signed, have the living will passed to the third and final witness, who also signs where indicated and fills in his or her address. Throughout this ceremony, you and all of the witnesses must remain together.

- The final step is for the Notary Public to sign in the space indicated. When this step is completed, your living will is a valid legal document. Have several copies made and, if appropriate, deliver a copy to your attending physician to have placed in your medical records file. You may also desire to give a copy to the person you have chosen as the executor of your will, a copy to your clergy, and a copy to your spouse or other trusted relative.

Some states require that you periodically re-sign your living will for it to remain valid. Please check with an attorney regarding the particular provisions in your state.

Living Will Declaration and Directive to Physicians
of _____

I, _____, willfully and voluntarily make known my desire that my life not be artificially prolonged under the circumstances set forth below, and, pursuant to any and all applicable laws in the State of _____, I declare that:

1. If at any time I should have an incurable injury, disease, or illness which has been certified as a terminal condition by my attending physician and one additional physician, both of whom have personally examined me, and such physicians have determined that there can be no recovery from such condition and my death is imminent, and where the application of life prolonging procedures would serve only to artificially prolong the dying process, I direct that such procedures be withheld or withdrawn, and that I be permitted to die naturally with only the administration of medication, the administration of nutrition, or the performance of any medical procedure deemed necessary to provide me with comfort, care, or to alleviate pain.

2. If at any time I should have been diagnosed as being in a persistent vegetative state which has been certified as incurable by my attending physician and one additional physician, both of whom have personally examined me, and such physicians have determined that there can be no recovery from such condition, and where the application of life prolonging procedures would serve only to artificially prolong the dying process, I direct that such procedures be withheld or withdrawn, and that I be permitted to die naturally with only the administration of medication, the administration of nutrition, or the performance of any medical procedure deemed necessary to provide me with comfort, care, or to alleviate pain.

3. In the absence of my ability to give directions regarding my treatment in the above situations, including directions regarding the use of such life prolonging procedures, it is my intention that this declaration shall be honored by my

family, my physician, and any court of law, as the final expression of my legal right to refuse medical and surgical treatment. I declare that I fully accept the consequences for such refusal.

4.   If I am diagnosed as pregnant, this document shall have no force and effect during my pregnancy.

5.   I understand the full importance of this declaration, and I am emotionally and mentally competent to make this declaration and Living Will. No person shall be in any way responsible for the making or placing into effect of this declaration and Living Will or for carrying out my express directions. I also understand that I may revoke this document at any time.

I publish and sign this Living Will and Directive to Physicians, consisting of _____ typewritten pages, on _____, 19 _____, and declare that I do so freely, for the purposes expressed, under no constraint or undue influence, and that I am of sound mind and of legal age.

_____
(Declarant's Signature)

_____
(Printed Name of Declarant)

On _____, 19 _____, in the presence of all of us, the above-named Declarant published and signed this Living Will and Directive to Physicians, and then at the Declarant's request, and in the Declarant's presence, and in each other's presence, we all signed below as witnesses, and we each declare, under penalty of perjury, that, to the best of our knowledge,

1.   The Declarant is personally known to me and, to the best of my knowledge, the Declarant signed this instrument freely, under no constraint or undue influence,

and is of sound mind and memory and legal age, and fully aware of the possible consequences of this action.

2.   I am at least 19 years of age and I am not related to the Declarant in any manner: by blood, marriage, or adoption.

3.   I am not the Declarant's attending physician, or a patient or employee of the Declarant's attending physician; or a patient, physician, or employee of the health care facility in which the Declarant is a patient, unless such person is required or allowed to witness the execution of this document by the laws of the state in which this document is executed.

4.   I am not entitled to any portion of the Declarant's estate on the Declarant's death under the laws of intestate succession of any state or country, nor under the Last Will and Testament of the Declarant or any Codicil to such Last Will and Testament.

5.   I have no claim against any portion of the Declarant's estate on the Declarant's death.

6.   I am not directly financially responsible for the Declarant's medical care.

7.   I did not sign the Declarant's signature for the Declarant or on the direction of the Declarant, nor have I been paid any fee for acting as a witness to the execution of this document.

_____
(Signature of Witness)

_____
(Printed name of Witness)

_____
(Signature of Witness)

_____
(Printed name of Witness)

_____
(Signature of Witness)

_____
(Printed name of Witness)

County of _____} SS.

State of _____}

On _____, 19 _____, before me personally appeared _____

_____, the Declarant, _____, the first witness, _____, the second witness, _____, the third witness, and, being first sworn on oath and under penalty of perjury, state that, in the presence of all the witnesses, the Declarant published and signed the above Living Will Declaration and Directive to Physicians, and then, at Declarant's request, and in the presence of the Declarant and of each other, each of the witnesses signed as witnesses, and stated that, to the best of their knowledge, the Declarant signed said Living Will Declaration and Directive to Physicians freely, under no constraint or undue influence, and is of sound mind and memory and legal age and fully aware of the potential consequences of this action. The witnesses further state that this affidavit is made at the direction of and in the presence of the Declarant.

_____
(Signature of Notary Public)

Notary Public, In and for the County of _____,

State of _____.

Revocation of your Living Will

All states which have recognized living wills have provided methods for the easy revocation of them. Since they provide authority to medical personnel to withhold life-support technology which will likely result in death to the patient, great care must be taken to insure that a change of mind by the patient is heeded.

If revocation of your living will is an important issue, please consult your state's law directly.

For the revocation of a living will, any one of the following methods of revocation is generally acceptable:

- Physical destruction of the living will, such as tearing, burning, or mutilating the document.

- A written revocation of the living will by you or by a person acting at your direction. A form for this is provided. You may use two witnesses on this form, although most states do not require the use of witnesses for the written revocation of a living will to be valid.

- An oral revocation in the presence of a witness who signs and dates a writing confirming a revocation. This oral declaration may take any manner. Most states allow for a person to revoke such a document by any indication (even non-verbal) of the intent to revoke a living will, regardless of their physical or mental condition.

To use the Revocation of Living Will form provided on the next page, simply fill in the appropriate information, retype the form, and sign it. In addition, your two witnesses may sign it at the same time.

Revocation of Living Will

I , _____ , am the Declarant and maker of a
Living Will and Directive to Physicians, dated _____, 19, __.
By this written revocation, I hereby entirely revoke such Living Will and Directive to
Physicians and intend that it no longer have any force or effect.

Dated _____, 19 _____.

_____
(Declarant's Signature)

_____
(Printed Name of Declarant)

_____
(Signature of Witness)

_____
(Printed name of Witness)

_____
(Signature of Witness)

_____
(Printed name of Witness)

_____
(Signature of Witness)

_____
(Printed name of Witness)

CHAPTER 7

LIVING TRUST

A *living trust* or revocable trust is a legal document which is used to pass your assets to your beneficiaries on your death. Thus, it accomplishes much the same results as a will. Like a will, it is revocable at any time during your life. Also like a will, it allows you to retain control over your assets during your life and affords no direct tax advantages. However, it does have a few advantages over a will and a few disadvantages, as well.

The main advantage to the use of a living trust instead of a will is that it allows your assets to be passed to your beneficiaries automatically upon your death, without any delay, probate, court intervention, or lawyer's fees. To many people, this very important advantage outweighs any disadvantages. Another advantage is that it is much more difficult to challenge a living trust in court than it is to challenge a will. Finally, a living trust is a more private document which only needs to be recorded with the county recorder in the event that real estate is transferred with such a trust.

Perhaps the most important disadvantage of the use of a living trust is the need to actually transfer to the trust all of the property intended to be put in trust. This requirement and the need to keep accurate trust records makes the actual mechanics of a living trust more complicated than simply preparing a will.

Even if you decide to use a living trust to pass your assets to your beneficiaries, you will also need to prepare a will. This is because regardless of your best efforts, you will not generally be able to name each and every item of property that you own. Without a will as a back-up, any property not named in the living trust will pass to your closest relatives or if there are none, the property may be forfeited to the state.

To create a living trust, you will first need to decide what property you wish to place in trust. To do this, you may use the property questionnaire that is provided in Chapter 5 for use with a will. Assets that are subject to being sold or discarded regularly shouldn't be put in the trust.

Next, you will need to decide who is to receive your assets upon your death. Again, you may use the beneficiary questionnaire which is included in Chapter 5. Finally, you will need to decide if you wish to retain all control over the trust. To achieve this end, you will name yourself as trustee.

Once you have created your living trust, you will need to actually transfer the ownership of all of the assets selected to the trust. This transfer may include obtaining a new title to your car, new bank accounts, and a new deed to any real estate. The new ownership will be in the name of the trust itself, with the name of the trustee specified: for example, *The Jane Smith Revocable Living Trust; Jane Smith, Trustee* might be the name on the deed or title.

On the following pages, are the following forms:

Living Trust: The information needed for this form is the name and address of the *grantor* (the one who is creating the trust), the date the trust will take effect, the name of the *trustee* (the one who will have control over the trust, usually the same as the grantor), the name of a successor trustee (usually a spouse, child of legal age, or trusted friend), the list of beneficiaries and their gifts, the name of the state in which you reside, and the signature of the grantor/trustee. The signature on this form should be notarized. This form of trust reserves the right to allow you to cancel or amend this trust at any time.

Schedule of Assets of Living Trust: On this form, you will include a listing of all of the property that you wish to transfer into the trust. This document should be attached to the living trust when completed.

Amendment to Living Trust: This form is used to make any changes to the living trust, for example, adding or deleting any of the property listed on the Schedule of Assets or changing a beneficiary. Simply fill in the name and address of the grantor/trustee and specify the changes to the trust. The signature on this document should also be notarized.

Revocation of Living Trust: This document is used whenever you desire to terminate the trust. You may do this at any time. To revoke your trust, simply fill in the name and address of the grantor/trustee and the date of the original trust. The signature on this document should also be notarized.

LIVING TRUST OF _____

I, _____, Grantor, residing at
_____, City of _____, State of _____
_____, declare and make this Living Trust on _____19 ___.

This trust will be known as the _____ Revocable
Living Trust. I, _____ will be trustee of this trust.
Upon my death or if I am unable to manage this trust and my financial affairs, then I
appoint _____, my _____, residing at___
_____, City of _____, State of _____, as
successor trustee, to serve without bond. In addition to any powers, authority, and discretion granted by law, I grant such Trustee and Successor Trustee any and all powers
to perform any acts, in his or her sole discretion and without court approval, for the
management and distribution of this trust.

This trust shall terminate twenty-one (21) years after death of the last specifically-
named beneficiary of this trust who was alive at the time of creation of this trust.

I reserve the right to change any or all of this trust at any time. The changes must be
written, notarized, and attached to this document to be valid. I also reserve the right to
cancel this trust at any time. A cancellation of this trust must be written, notarized, and
attached to this document to be valid.

I transfer ownership to this trust of all of the assets which are listed on the attached
Schedule of Assets of Living Trust, which is specifically made a part of this trust. I reserve the right to add or delete any of these assets at any time. Any additions of dele-
tions must be written, notarized, and attached to this document to be valid.

Upon my death, the successor trustee shall pay my valid debts, last expenses and estate taxes from the residue of this trust and shall distribute the trust assets as follows:

I give _____

_____

to _____,

who is my _____, or if not surviving to_____

_____, who is my _____.

I give _____

_____

to _____,

who is my _____, or if not surviving to_____

_____, who is my _____.

This trust was created on the date noted above and will be governed under the laws of the State of _____.

_____
(Signature of Grantor)

_____
(Printed name of Grantor)

State of _____
County of _____

On _____, 19 __, _____ came before me personally and, under oath, stated that he/she is the person described in the above document and he/she signed the above document in my presence.

_____
(Notary signature)

Notary Public, for the County of _____, State of _____

My commission expires: _____

SCHEDULE OF ASSETS OF LIVING TRUST

This Schedule of Assets of Living Trust is attached and made part of the Revocable Living Trust of _____, which was created on _____, 19 _____. The following assets are made part of this Living Trust:

AMENDMENT OF LIVING TRUST

This Amendment of Living Trust is made on _____, 19 ___, by _____, Grantor, residing at _____, City of_____, State of _____, to the Living Trust dated _____, 19 ___.

The Grantor modifies the original Living Trust as follows:

All other terms and conditions of the original Living Trust remain in effect without modification. This Amendment, including the original Living Trust, is the entire Living Trust as of this date. The Grantor has signed this Amendment on the date specified at the beginning of this Amendment.

_____
(Signature of Grantor)

_____
(Printed name of Grantor)

State of _____

County of _____

On _____, 19 ___, _____ came before me personally and, under oath, stated that he/she is the person described in the above document and he/she signed the above document in my presence.

_____
(Notary signature)

Notary Public, for the County of _____, State of _____

My commission expires: _____

REVOCATION OF LIVING TRUST

I, _____, residing at _____, City

of _____, State of _____, revoke the Living Trust dated

_____, 19___.

Dated: _____, 19 _____

_____
(Signature of grantor of living trust)

State of _____

County of _____

On _____, 19 ___, _____ came before me

personally and, under oath, stated that he/she is the person described in the above doc-

ument and he/she signed the above document in my presence.

_____
(Notary signature)

Notary Public, for the County of _____, State of _____

My commission expires: _____

CHAPTER 8

PRE-MARITAL AGREEMENT

A *pre-marital* (or pre-nuptial) agreement is a specific type of contract between two persons who are intending marriage. It is entered into in order to spell out the effect of their forthcoming marriage on their individual property and financial situations. A pre-marital agreement is, essentially, an agreement to alter the general legal effect of marriage.

In the United States, there are two general sets of rules that apply to the ownership of marital property. Under the laws of the *community property* states of Arizona, California, Idaho, Louisiana, Nevada, New Mexico, Texas, Washington, and Wisconsin, all property owned by spouses is divided into two distinct classes: separate property and community property. Separate property is generally described as consisting of three types of property:

- Property that each spouse owned individually prior to their marriage;
- Property that each spouse acquired by individual gift, either before or during the marriage (Gifts given to both spouses together or gifts given by one spouse to the other are generally considered community property); and
- Property that each spouse acquired by inheritance (legally referred to as "by bequest, descent, or devise"), either before or during the marriage.

In community property states, all marital property that is not separate property is referred to as community property. This includes anything that either spouse earned or acquired at any time during the marriage that is not separate property. The property acquired during the marriage is considered community property regardless of whose name may be on the title to the property, and regardless of who actually paid for the property (unless it was paid for entirely with one spouse's separate property funds and remains separate).

The other 41 states follow what is referred to as the *common law* method of marital property ownership. It has distinct similarities to the community property system, and yet is different in many respects. In common law jurisdictions, certain marital property is subject to division by the judge upon divorce. Which property is subject to division varies somewhat from state to state but generally follows two basic patterns. The most common method of classifying property in common law states closely parallels the method used in community property states. Property is divided into two basic classes: *separate* or *non-marital* property and *marital* property. What constitutes property in each class is very similar to the definitions in community property states. This method of property division is termed *equitable distribution*.

The second method for distribution which is used in several states is to make *all* of a couple's property subject to division upon divorce. Regardless of whether it was obtained by gift, by inheritance, or was brought into the marriage, and regardless of whose name is on the title or deed, the property may be apportioned to either spouse depending upon the decision of the judge. There is no differentiation between marital, non-marital, or separate property. The property is still divided on a basis which attempts to achieve a general fairness, but all of a couple's property is available for such distribution. Some states use a hybrid of the two above methods.

The use of a pre-marital agreement can effectively alter the classification of a spouse's property which is brought into a marriage. Thus, with the use of a pre-marital agreement, the potential spouses can agree that all of their property which they bring into a marriage will remain as their own separate property throughout the marriage and will not be subject to any division upon eventual divorce. A pre-marital agreement of this type makes a couple's property rights regarding property brought to a marriage similar to that of community property states and those common law states which follow similar laws regarding separate and marital property.

The pre-marital agreement which is contained in this book also provides that the potential spouses waive forever any and all rights that they may have to alimony or claims of support which would have to be provided out of any property which is in existence as of the date of the pre-marital agreement. Any property which is acquired during the marriage, however, will remain subject to division in the event of a divorce.

Following is a detailed property questionnaire which should be used to specify what property each potential spouse actually owns prior to the marriage. This questionnaire should then be used to fill in the information detailing the property ownership on the pre-marital agreement.

PRE-MARITAL PROPERTY QUESTIONNAIRE

REAL ESTATE

Do you own your own home? _____

    If (YES): What is the address? _____

When was it purchased? _____

Whose name(s) is on the deed? _____

What was the original purchase price? . . . . $ _____

What is the present market value? . . . .$ _____

How much is left unpaid on the mortgage? . . . .$ _____

What is the equity (market value minus mortgage balance)? . . . $ _____

How much is the monthly mortgage payment? . . . .$ _____

Have there been any major improvements made since its purchase? _____

    (If YES): When were the improvements made? _____

    How much did they cost? . . . . $ _____

Here list the actual legal description of the home (taken directly off the deed or mortgage): _____

_____

Other Real Estate:

What is the address? _____

When was it purchased? _____

Whose name(s) is on the deed? _____

What was the original purchase price? . . . . $ _____

What is the present market value? . . . .$ _____

How much is left unpaid on the mortgage? . . . .$ _____

What is the equity (market value minus mortgage balance)? . . . $ _____

How much is the monthly mortgage payment? . . . .$ _____

How much are the taxes? . . . . $ _____

Is there any rental income? . . . .$ _____

Have there been any major improvements made since its purchase? _____

    (If YES): When were the improvements made? _____

    How much did they cost? . . . . $ _____

Here list the actual legal description of the home (taken directly off the deed or mortgage): _____

_____

PERSONAL PROPERTY:

Bank Accounts:

Savings:

    Bank _____ Account # _____

    Owner _____ Amount $ _____

Checking:
    Bank _____ Account # _____
    Owner _____ Amount $ _____

Certificates of Deposit:
    Bank _____ Account # _____
    Owner _____ Amount $ _____

Money Market Accounts:
    Bank _____ Account # _____
    Owner _____ Amount $ _____

Stocks:
    Company _____ CUSIP # _____
    Owner _____ # Shares _____
    Annual Dividend $ _____ Value $ _____

    Company _____ CUSIP # _____
    Owner _____ # Shares _____
    Annual Dividend $ _____ Value $ _____

Bonds:
    Company _____ CUSIP # _____
    Owner _____ # Shares _____
    Annual Interest $ _____ Value $ _____
    Company _____ CUSIP # _____
    Owner _____ # Shares _____
    Annual Interest $ _____ Value $ _____

Other Personal Property:
    Car #1: Year _____ Make and model _____
    When purchased? _____ Whose name on title?_____
    License plate # and state: _____ Payment $ _____
    Amount of car loan unpaid $ _____ Value $ _____

    Car #2: Year _____ Make and model _____
    When purchased? _____ Whose name on title?_____
    License plate # and state: _____ Payment $ _____
    Amount of car loan unpaid $ _____ Value $ _____

    Other vehicles (boats, campers, motorcycles, etc): describe _____

    _____
    When purchased? _____ Value $ _____

Stereo: describe _____

Who has possession? _____ Value $ _____

Jewelry: describe _____

When purchased? _____ Value $ _____

Tools: describe _____

When purchased? _____ Value $ _____

Sporting Goods: describe _____

When purchased? _____ Value $ _____

Furniture: describe _____

When purchased? _____ Value $ _____

Appliances: describe _____

When purchased? _____ Value $ _____

Other property: describe _____

When purchased? _____ Value $ _____

Other property: describe _____

When purchased? _____ Value $ _____

Other property: describe _____

When purchased? _____ Value $ _____

Business Assets: (Corporations, Partnerships, Proprietorships)

Description: _____

Location: _____

When purchased? _____ Value $ _____

Description: _____

Location: _____

When purchased? _____ Value $ _____

Retirement/Pension/Profit-sharing/Stock Option Plans:

IRA Accounts:

Bank or broker _____ Account # _____

When purchased? _____ Amount $ _____

Retirement Funds:
    Company _____ Account # _____
    When purchased? _____ Value $ _____

Profit-sharing Plan:
    Company _____ Account # _____
    When purchased? _____ Value $ _____

Stock Option Plan:
    Company _____ Account # _____
    When purchased? _____ Value $ _____

Insurance:
    Life Insurance:
        Company: _____
        On whose life: _____ Beneficiary: _____
        Premium: $ _____ Cash Value $ _____

    Medical Insurance:
        Company: _____ Amount $ _____
        On whom: _____ Premium: $ _____

    Disability Insurance:
        Company: _____ Amount $ _____
        On whom: _____ Premium: $ _____

    Auto Insurance:
        Company: _____ Amount $ _____
        Which car?: _____ Premium: $ _____

    Homeowner's Insurance:
        Company: _____ Amount $ _____
        Property address _____
        _____ Premium: $ _____

    Other Insurance:
        Company: _____ Amount $ _____
        What purpose? _____ Premium: $ _____

PRE-MARITAL AGREEMENT

This agreement is made on the _____ day of _____,
19 _____, between _____, residing at_____
_____, City of _____, County of _____
_____, State of _____, and _____
_____, residing at _____, City of _____
_____, County of _____, State of _____.

We intend to be married on the _____ day of _____, 19 __, in
the City of _____, County of _____, State of _____.

We both desire to settle by agreement the ownership rights of all of our property that
we currently own and our rights to alimony, spousal support, or maintenance.

THEREFORE, in consideration of our mutual promises, and other good and valuable
consideration, we agree as follows:

We agree that the following property shall be the sole and separate property of
_____:

_____
_____
_____
_____

We also agree that the following property shall be the sole and separate property of
_____:

_____
_____
_____
_____

We agree that the above listed property shall remain their own separate and personal estate, including any rents, interest or profits which may be earned on such property. This property shall forever remain free and clear of any claim by the other person. Each person shall have the right to control, sell, or give away their own separate property as if they were not married. We both agree to waive any rights or claims that we may have now or in the future to receive any distribution of any of the other's separate property in the event of divorce or dissolution of marriage.

However, in the event of divorce or dissolution of marriage, any marital property which is acquired after marriage will be subject to division, either by agreement between us or by a judicial determination.

After careful consideration of our circumstances and all of the other terms of this agreement, we both agree to waive any rights or claims that we may have now or in the future to receive alimony, maintenance, or spousal support from the other in the event of divorce or dissolution of marriage. We both fully understand that we are forever giving up any rights that we may have to alimony, maintenance, or spousal support in the event of divorce or dissolution of marriage.

We have prepared this agreement cooperatively and each of us has fully and honestly disclosed to the other the extent of our assets.

We each understand that we have the right to representation by independent counsel. We each fully understand our rights and we each consider the terms of this agreement to be fair and reasonable.

Both of us agree to execute and deliver any documents, make any endorsements, and do any and all acts that may be necessary or convenient to carry out all of the terms of this agreement.

We agree that this document is intended to be the full and entire pre-marital agreement between us and should be interpreted and governed by the laws of the State of

_____.

We also agree that every provision of this agreement is expressly made binding upon the heirs, assigns, executors, administrators, successors in interest, and representatives of each of us.

Signed and dated this day _____ of _____ , 19_____ .

_____
[Signature]

_____
[Witness signature]

_____
[Witness signature]

_____
[Signature]

_____
[Witness signature]

_____
[Witness signature]

State of _____

SS.

County of _____

On _____, 19 ___, _____ and _____ personally came before me and, being duly sworn, did state that they are the persons described in the above document and that they signed the above document in my presence as a free and voluntary act for the purposes stated .

_____
(Notary signature)

Notary Public, for the County of _____

State of _____

My Commission expires _____

CHAPTER 9

MARITAL SETTLEMENT AGREEMENT

For many people, separation is the first step in the divorce process. You and your spouse may decide to separate under the terms of a *marital settlement agreement* (or separation agreement) or you may wish to seek an actual legal separation from a court. A legal court-ordered separation is slightly different than a separation by agreement. Legal court-ordered separations are not provided for in all states. However, a marital separation by mutual agreement is recognized and honored in every state. Neither a court-ordered separation nor a separation agreement will legally end the marriage. Only a divorce can do that.

The marital settlement agreement that you prepare using this book will cover all of the terms of an eventual divorce. Included in your agreement will be all of the decisions that you and your spouse make regarding how your property and bills are divided, and whether either of you should get alimony. This agreement, when signed by you and your spouse, will become a valid legal contract that will be enforceable in a court of law if either you or your spouse violate its terms. The marital settlement agreement in this book is designed only for use by couples who do *not* have any children.

There are two general sets of rules that apply to the division of property upon divorce in the United States. There are nine *community property* states which essentially view all of the property obtained during a marriage as being owned equally by the spouses. The community property states are: Arizona, California, Idaho, Louisiana, Nevada, New Mexico, Texas, Washington, and Wisconsin. All of the other states are known as *common law* states. In these states, upon divorce a couple's property is subject to being divided on a more or less fair or equitable basis.

The law in community property states generally holds that all property which a couple obtained while they were married should be shared equally by the spouses. Marriage was viewed essentially as an equal business partnership. Property owned by spouses in these states is divided into two distinct classes: separate property and community property. Separate property is generally described as consisting of three types of property:

• Property that each spouse owned individually prior to their marriage;

• Property that each spouse acquired by individual gift, either before or during the marriage (Gifts given to both spouses together or gifts given by one spouse to the other are generally considered community property); and

• Property that each spouse acquired by inheritance (legally referred to as "by bequest, descent, or devise"), either before or during the marriage.

In community property states, all marital property that is not separate property is referred to as community property. This includes anything that either spouse earned or acquired at any time during the marriage that is not separate property. The property acquired during the marriage is considered community property regardless of whose name may be on the title to the property, and regardless of who actually paid for the property (unless it was paid for entirely with one spouse's separate property funds and remains separate). All of a couple's bills and obligations that are incurred during a marriage are also considered community property and are to be divided equally upon divorce. (A few states, however, consider educational loans for one spouse to be a separate debt and not to be shared by the other spouse upon divorce).

Most community property states require an equal division of all community property or start with a presumption that an *equal* division is the fairest method, although even these states will allow some leeway from an exact 50-50 division depending on the facts of the case. The remaining community property states provide for an *equitable* division of the community property. In this situation, equitable is defined to mean fair and just.

In the other 41 common law-type states, there are two methods for property division. There are states that abide by what is known as an *equitable distribution* method of property division. It has distinct similarities to the community property system, and yet is different in many respects. In equitable distribution jurisdictions, certain marital property is subject to division by the judge upon divorce. Which property is subject to division varies somewhat from state to state but generally follows two basic patterns. The most common method of classifying property in equitable distribution states closely parallels the method used in community property states. Property is divided into two basic classes: *separate* or *non-marital* property and *marital* property. What constitutes property in each class is very similar to the definitions in community property states.

112

The second method for distribution which is used in several states is to make *all* of a couple's property subject to division upon divorce. Regardless of whether it was obtained by gift, by inheritance, or was brought into the marriage, and regardless of whose name is on the title or deed, the property may be apportioned to either spouse depending upon the decision of the judge. There is no differentiation between marital, non-marital, or separate property. The property is still divided on a basis which attempts to achieve a general fairness, but all of a couple's property is available for such distribution. Some states use a hybrid of the two above methods.

On the next few pages you will fill out a several questionnaires, checklists, and worksheets that cover basic personal information as well as information regarding your property and incomes. By filling in these questionnaires, you will be able to have in front of you all of the necessary and relevant information for preparing your agreement. After the questionnaires and worksheet, you will find a Marital Settlement Agreement which may be filled in with the information from the questionnaires and worksheets. Finally, there is a Financial Statement form. Each spouse will need to fill in a copy of this form and the completed forms should be attached to the completed Marital Settlement Agreement. If you and your spouse have children or if further information regarding marital settlement agreements or divorce is necessary, please consult *"Divorce Yourself: The National No-Fault Divorce Kit"*, by Daniel Sitarz (Nova Publishing Company). If additional advice is required, please consult a competent attorney.

PRELIMINARY QUESTIONNAIRE

Wife's Full Name:_____

Wife's Former or Maiden Name:_____

Does Wife Desire to Use Her Former Name?_____

Wife's Social Security #:_____

Wife's Date of Birth:_____

Wife's Present Address:_____

Wife's Future Address (if known):_____

Date Future Address Valid:_____

Wife's Present Phone #:_____

Wife's Present Occupation:_____

Wife's Present Place of Employment:_____

Wife's General Health:_____

Was Wife Previously Married?_____

If YES, how was marriage terminated? (divorce, death, etc.):_____

Husband's Full Name:_____

Husband's Social Security #:_____

Husband's Date of Birth:_____

Husband's Present Address:_____

Husband's Future Address (if known):_____

Date Future Address Valid:_____

Husband's Present Phone #:_____

Husband's Present Occupation:_____

Husband's Present Place of Employment:_____

Was Husband Previously Married?_____

If YES, how was marriage terminated? (divorce, death, etc.):_____

Full Address(es) Where Husband and Wife Have Lived During the Past 12 Months:_____
_____

Date of Marriage:_____

Place of Marriage:_____

Have you and your spouse physically separated?_____

If YES, on what date did you separate?_____

Have you previously separated at any time?_____

If YES, on what dates and for how long?_____

DOCUMENT CHECKLIST

- Wife's Birth Certificate: (Mandatory)
- Husband's Birth Certificate: (Mandatory)
- Immigration and Naturalization Documents: (Mandatory if applicable)
- Marriage License: (Mandatory)
- Any Written Agreements between Wife and Husband: (Mandatory)
- Social Security Cards:
- Personal Financial Statements:
- Documents relating to any prior marriage: (Settlement Agreements, Divorce documents, Death Certificate, etc.)
- All documents relating to income, expenses, and property:
- Federal, state, and local income tax returns:
- Payroll stubs and W-2 Forms:
- Records regarding any other income:
- Records regarding monthly living expenses:
- Pension and retirement plan policies and records:
- Stock option and profit-sharing plans and records:
- Business tax returns (Corporate, partnership, or sole proprietorship):
- Business financial statements:
- Deeds to any real estate:
- Mortgages or deeds of trust for any real estate:
- Copies of any leases:
- Checking account statements:
- Savings account statements and passbooks:
- Certificates of Deposit:
- Stock certificates and bonds:
- Securities stockbroker account statements:
- Titles to cars, boats, motorcycles, etc.:
- Any outstanding loan documents:
- Credit card records:
- Records of any other debts:
- Life insurance policies:
- Health insurance policies:
- Auto insurance policies:
- Homeowner's insurance policy:
- Other insurance policies:
- Inventory of contents of safety deposit boxes:
- Appraisals of any property:
- Records of any gifts or inheritances:
- Any other important documents:

PROPERTY QUESTIONNAIRE

REAL ESTATE
Family Home:

Do you lease a home or apartment? _____

    If (YES): How much time is left on the lease? _____

Do you own your own home? _____

    If (YES): What is the address? _____

When was it purchased? _____

    (Was this before or during the marriage?) _____

Whose money was used for down payment? _____

Whose name(s) is on the deed? _____

How much was the down payment? . . . .$ _____

What was the original purchase price? . . . .$ _____

What is the present market value? . . . .$ _____

How much is left unpaid on the mortgage? . . . .$ _____

What is the equity (market value minus mortgage balance)? . . . $ _____

How much is the monthly mortgage payment? . . . .$ _____

How much are the taxes? . . . .$ _____

How much is the homeowner's insurance? . . . .$ _____

Have there been any major improvements made since its purchase? _____

    (If YES): When were the improvements made? _____

    How much did they cost? . . . . $ _____

    Whose money was used? _____

Here list the actual legal description of the home (taken directly off the deed or mortgage): _____

_____

Other Real Estate:

What is the address? _____

When was it purchased? _____

    (Was this before or during the marriage?) _____

Whose money was used for down payment? _____

Whose name(s) is on the deed? _____

How much was the down payment? . . . .$ _____

What was the original purchase price? . . . .$ _____

What is the present market value? . . . .$ _____

How much is left unpaid on the mortgage? . . . .$ _____

What is the equity (market value minus mortgage balance)? . . . $ _____

How much is the monthly mortgage payment? . . . .$ _____

How much are the taxes? . . . .$ _____

How much is the insurance? . . . .$ _____

Is there any rental income? . . . .$ _____

Have there been any major improvements made since its purchase? _____
      (If YES): When were the improvements made? _____
      How much did they cost? . . . . $ _____
      Whose money was used? _____
Here list the actual legal description of the home (taken directly off the deed or mortgage): _____
_____

PERSONAL PROPERTY: (The term "owner" refers to the person in whose name the account, stock, bond, etc. is held. If jointly held, write "joint".)

Bank Accounts:

Savings:
    Bank _____ Account # _____
    Owner _____ Amount $ _____

Checking:
    Bank _____ Account # _____
    Owner _____ Amount $ _____

Certificates of Deposit:
    Bank _____ Account # _____
    Owner _____ Amount $ _____

Money Market Accounts:
    Bank _____ Account # _____
    Owner _____ Amount $ _____

Stocks:

Company _____ CUSIP # _____
    Owner _____ # Shares _____
    Annual Dividend $ _____ Value $ _____

Company _____ CUSIP # _____
    Owner _____ # Shares _____
    Annual Dividend $ _____ Value $ _____

Bonds:

Company _____ CUSIP # _____
    Owner _____ # Shares _____
    Annual Interest $ _____ Value $ _____

Company _____ CUSIP # _____
    Owner _____ # Shares _____
    Annual Interest $ _____ Value $ _____

Names and addresses of you and your spouse's stockbrokers:

_____
_____

Income Tax:

Did you file a joint return for the last tax year? _____
Is there a tax or refund due? _____
    How much State? . . . .$ _____
    How much Federal? . . . .$ _____
    How much Local? . . . .$ _____

Other Personal Property:

Car #1: Year _____ Make and model _____
Who has possession? _____ Whose name on title?_____
License plate # and state: _____ Payment $ _____
Amount of car loan unpaid $ _____ Value $ _____

Car #2: Year _____ Make and model _____
Who has possession? _____ Whose name on title?_____
License plate # and state: _____ Payment $ _____
Amount of car loan unpaid $ _____ Value $ _____

Other vehicles (boats, campers, motorcycles, etc): describe _____
_____
Who has possession? _____ Value $ _____

Stereo: describe _____
Who has possession? _____ Value $ _____

Jewelry: describe _____
Who has possession? _____ Value $ _____

Tools: describe _____
Who has possession? _____ Value $ _____

Sporting Goods: describe _____
Who has possession? _____ Value $ _____

Furniture: describe _____
Who has possession? _____ Value $ _____

Appliances: describe _____
Who has possession? _____ Value $ _____

Other property: describe _____
Who has possession? _____ Value $ _____

Other property: describe _____
Who has possession? _____ Value $ _____

Business Assets: (Corporations, Partnerships, Proprietorships)

Description: _____
Location: _____
Who has ownership? _____ Value $ _____

Description: _____
Location: _____
Who has ownership? _____ Value $ _____

Retirement/Pension/Profit-sharing/Stock Option Plans:

IRA Accounts:
    Bank or broker _____ Account # _____
    Owner _____ Amount $ _____

Retirement Funds:
    Company _____ Account # _____
    Whose fund? _____ Value $ _____

Profit-sharing Plan:
    Company _____ Account # _____
    Whose fund? _____ Value $ _____

Stock Option Plan:
    Company _____ Account # _____
    Whose fund? _____ Value $ _____

Pension Plan:
    Company _____ Account # _____
    Whose fund? _____ Value $ _____

Insurance:

Life Insurance:
Company: _____
On whose life: _____ Beneficiary: _____
Premium: $ _____ Cash Value $ _____

Company: _____
On whose life: _____ Beneficiary: _____
Premium: $ _____ Cash Value $ _____

Medical Insurance:
Company: _____ Amount $ _____
On whom: _____ Premium: $ _____

Company: _____ Amount $ _____
On whom: _____ Premium: $ _____

Disability Insurance:
Company: _____ Amount $ _____
On whom: _____ Premium: $ _____

Company: _____ Amount $ _____
On whom: _____ Premium: $ _____

Auto Insurance:
Company: _____ Amount $ _____
Which car?: _____ Premium: $ _____

Company: _____ Amount $ _____
Which car?: _____ Premium: $ _____

Homeowner's Insurance:
Company: _____ Amount $ _____
Property address _____
_____ Premium: $ _____

Other Insurance:
Company: _____ Amount $ _____
What purpose? _____ Premium: $ _____

Separate Property*:*

List all specific property owned prior to marriage that is still owned (note who owns each item and its value). List property here even if listed previously.

      Description _____

      Owner _____ Value $ _____

      Description _____

      Owner _____ Value $ _____

      Description _____

      Owner _____ Value $ _____

List all specific property received by gift or inheritance that is still owned (note who owns each item and its value). List property here even if listed previously.

      Description _____

      Owner _____ Value $ _____

      Description _____

      Owner _____ Value $ _____

Bills and Debts:

Credit Cards:

      Name of Company: _____

      Reason for debt: _____

      In whose name: _____

      Monthly payment: $ _____ Balance due $ _____

      Name of Company: _____

      Reason for debt: _____

      In whose name: _____

      Monthly payment: $ _____ Balance due $ _____

Other debts:

      Name of Company: _____

      Reason for debt: _____

      In whose name: _____

      Monthly payment: $ _____ Balance due $ _____

PROPERTY WORKSHEET

Separate Property of Spouse #1:

Description _____ Value $ _____
Description _____ Value $ _____
Description _____ Value $ _____
Description _____ Value $ _____
Description _____ Value $ _____
Description _____ Value $ _____
Description _____ Value $ _____
Description _____ Value $ _____
Description _____ Value $ _____

Total of Separate Property (Spouse #1): . . . . $_____

Separate Property of Spouse #2:

Description _____ Value $_____
Description _____ Value $_____
Description _____ Value $_____
Description _____ Value $_____
Description _____ Value $_____
Description _____ Value $_____
Description _____ Value $_____
Description _____ Value $_____
Description _____ Value $_____

Total of Separate Property (Spouse #1): . . . . $_____

Marital Property of Both Spouses:

Real estate:_____ Value $ _____
Auto:_____ Value $ _____
Furniture: _____ Value $ _____
Cash:_____ Value $ _____
Auto: _____ Value $ _____
Jewelry: _____ Value $ _____
Tools: _____ Value $ _____
Stocks: _____ Value $ _____
Bonds: _____ Value $ _____
Other : _____ Value $ _____

A.   Total Amount of Marital Property: . . . .$_____

Marital Bills and Obligations:

Creditor: _____ Balance $ _____
Creditor: _____ Balance $ _____
Creditor: _____ Balance $ _____
Creditor: _____ Balance $ _____
Creditor: _____ Balance $ _____
Creditor: _____ Balance $ _____
Creditor: _____ Balance $ _____

B. Total Amount of Marital Bills: . . . .$ _____

Value Of Marital Property To Be Divided:

Total Amount of Marital Property (A): . . . .$ _____
Minus (-) Total Amount of Marital Bills (B): . . . .$ _____
Equals (=) Total Value to be Divided (C) [A - B = C]: . . . .$ _____

Approximate Value to Each (1/2 or C/2): . . . . $ _____

Agreed Share of Marital Property and Bills for Each Spouse:

Spouse #1:
Description:_____ Value: $ _____
Description:_____ Value: $ _____
Description:_____ Value: $ _____
Description:_____ Value: $ _____
Description:_____ Value: $ _____
Description:_____ Value: $ _____
Description:_____ Value: $ _____
Description:_____ Value: $ _____

TOTAL MARITAL PROPERTY Spouse #1: $ _____

Spouse #2:
Description:_____ Value: $ _____
Description:_____ Value: $ _____
Description:_____ Value: $ _____
Description:_____ Value: $ _____
Description:_____ Value: $ _____
Description:_____ Value: $ _____
Description:_____ Value: $ _____
Description:_____ Value: $ _____

TOTAL MARITAL PROPERTY Spouse #2: $ _____

ALIMONY QUESTIONNAIRE

The right to alimony in a modern divorce setting is no longer the sole province of the wife. Both spouses are considered to be equally eligible to receive alimony under the laws in all states. Alimony awards are not commonly awarded to either spouse, however. Such awards are only made in approximately 15% of all divorces. Spousal support after marriage is definitely not common, and you should approach your discussion of alimony with this fact firmly in mind. In certain situations, however, alimony is an important and valuable right. Please note that the marital settlement agreement in this book provides for *no alimony for either spouse.*

The approach that most courts have taken to making decisions about alimony has been to review a list of factors that are relevant to support of a spouse. Other than these lists of factors, there have generally been no set guidelines provided for use in determining the actual amount of alimony to award. If you and your spouse can not reach an agreement regarding alimony you may need to seek legal assistance in order to protect your rights to sufficient future alimony. In cases where you decide that alimony is not necessary, a lawyer is generally not needed. However, If your marriage has been of long duration and one of you will be reasonably incapable of self-support in the future, it is recommended that you seek the assistance of a competent attorney. In such cases, alimony may be the most important economic factor in the divorce and may be the only method by which a non-self-sufficient spouse will be able to achieve a secure life. In cases where alimony will be a major factor and constitute the primary economic support for one spouse, many other factors (for example: cost-of-living adjustments and long-term tax consequences) become important. The advice of a lawyer is generally necessary in such situations. Please note that all of the information that is listed on both the Property Questionnaire and Worksheet is relevant to any discussion of alimony and may be necessary for filling in this questionnaire. Please refer to those forms when necessary.

How long have you been married? _____

Are you presently employed? _____

    If YES, where? _____

        _____

        For how long? _____

        What rate of pay? $ _____

        What education necessary? _____

Prior to that what was your former job? _____

    Where? _____

        _____

    For how long? _____

    What rate of pay $ _____

    What education necessary? _____

Prior to that what was your former job? _____
    Where? _____
    _____

    For how long? _____
    What rate of pay $ _____
    What education necessary? _____
Prior to that what was your former job? _____
    Where? _____
    _____

    For how long? _____
    What rate of pay $ _____
    What education necessary? _____
If you are not now employed when was your last job? _____
    Where? _____
    For how long? _____
    What rate of pay $ _____
    What education necessary? _____
Were you employed at the time of your marriage? _____
    Where? _____
    _____

    For how long? _____
    What rate of pay $ _____
    What education necessary? _____
What was the level of education that you had attained at the time of your marriage? _____
_____

What level of education have you attained now? _____
What job skills, training, or experience did you have at the time of your marriage? _____

What job skills, training, or experience do you now have? _____
_____

What is your usual occupation? _____
What will be your monthly income at the time of your separation? $ _____
What will be your monthly expenses at the time of your separation? $ _____
What will be the value of your property at the time of your separation? $ _____
How long would it take you to achieve the education or skills necessary to be able to in-
    dividually attain the standard of living that you enjoyed during your marriage? ___
_____

At any time during your marriage, did your spouse attend college or a special or profes-
    sional training course? _____
Did you sacrifice any career opportunities in order to allow your spouse to attend school
    or achieve success in his or her occupation? _____
Do you feel that you will be able to be self-sufficient after your divorce? _____
_____

125

Do you anticipate any unusual expenses or circumstances in the near future which may
      affect your ability to become self-supporting? _____

Do you and your spouse have any type of written pre-marital agreement? _____

      (If YES, what are the details that relate to alimony?) _____

_____

Do you feel that you deserve alimony? _____

      If YES, how much? $ _____

      Should it be paid in a lump-sum? _____

      Should it be paid in monthly payments? _____

            If YES, how long should the payments continue? _____

Preparing and Signing your Marital Settlement Agreement

1. As you prepare the marital settlement agreement, you should have before your all of the questionnaires and worksheets which you have completed. Make a photo-copy of the entire agreement as set forth in this book. Fill in the names, addresses, and marital information as called for in the first two paragraphs of the document.

2. Using your Property Worksheet, fill in the description of the property which is to be the wife's, free and clear. Then fill in the property which is to be the husband's. After this, fill in the bills or debts which the wife is to pay and those which the husband is to pay.

3. Decide who is to get the tax refund for the current year and who will pay any of the taxes due. If the wife desires to be known by her former name, insert that name in the appropriate blank. Finally, insert the name of the state which you are living in, or if living in separate states, the name of the state in which you lived as a married couple.

4. There are various other marital settlement agreement issues which are included in order for your agreement to have the necessary legal force. These standard legal phrases are important and should not be altered. They cover the following points:

- That you both want the terms of your marital settlement agreement to be the basis for a court order in the event of a divorce;

- That you both have prepared complete and honest Financial Statements and they are attached to your agreement;

- That you both know that you have the right to see your own lawyers and that you both understand your legal rights;

- That you both will sign any necessary documents;

- That you both intend that your agreement is the full statement of your rights and responsibilities; and

- That your agreement will be binding on any future representatives of yours.

5. Finally, the entire document should be re-typed on clean letter-sized paper and both spouses should sign the agreement in the presence of a notary public and two witnesses.

MARITAL SETTLEMENT AGREEMENT

This agreement is made on the _____ day of _____, 19 ___, _____betwe en _____, the Wife, residing at _____, City of _____, County of _____, State of _____ _____, and _____, the Husband, residing at _____City of _____, County of _____, State of _____.

We were married on the _____ day of _____, 19 _____, in the City of _____, County of _____, State of _____.

As a result of disputes and serious difficulties, we sincerely believe that our marriage is irretrievably broken and that there is no possible chance for reconciliation. As a result of irreconcilable disputes and serious differences, we have separated and are now living apart and intend to continue to remain permanently apart. We both desire to settle by agreement all of our marital affairs, including the division of all of our property and bills, and our rights to alimony, spousal support, or maintenance.

THEREFORE, in consideration of our mutual promises, and other good and valuable consideration, we agree as follows:

We both desire and agree to permanently live separate and apart from each other, as if we were single, according to the terms of this agreement. We each agree not to annoy, harass, or interfere with the other in any manner.

We agree that the following property shall be the sole and separate property of the Wife, and the Husband transfers and quit-claims any interest that he may have in this property to the Wife:

_____

_____

_____

We also agree that the following property shall be the sole and separate property of the Husband, and the Wife transfers and quit-claims any interest that she may have in this property to the Husband:

_____

_____

_____

We agree that the Wife shall pay and indemnify and hold the Husband harmless from the following debts:

_____

_____

_____

We agree that the Husband shall pay and indemnify and hold the Wife harmless from the following debts:

_____

_____

_____

We also agree not to incur any new debts or obligations for which the other may be liable.

After careful consideration of our circumstances and all of the other terms of this agreement, we both agree to waive any rights or claims that we may have now or in the future to receive alimony, maintenance, or spousal support from the other. We both fully understand that we are forever giving up any rights that we may have to alimony, maintenance, or spousal support.

We both agree that neither of us shall remain as the beneficiary on any insurance policy carried by the other.

We both agree that we will cooperate in the filing of any necessary tax returns. We also agree that any tax refunds for the current year will be the property of the _____ and that any taxes due for the current tax year will be paid by the _____.

We both agree to file a joint income tax return for the current year.

We both agree that, in the event of divorce or dissolution of marriage, the Wife desires to and shall have the right to be known by the name of _____ _____.

We both desire that, in the event of our divorce or dissolution of marriage, this marital settlement agreement be approved and merged and incorporated into any subsequent decree or judgement for divorce or dissolution of marriage and that, by the terms of the judgement or decree, we both be ordered to comply with the terms of this agreement, but that this agreement survive.

We have prepared this agreement cooperatively and each of us has fully and honestly disclosed to the other the extent of our assets, income, and finances. We have each completed Financial Statements which are attached and incorporated by reference.

We each understand that we have the right to representation by independent counsel. We each fully understand our rights and we each consider the terms of this agreement to be fair and reasonable.

Both of us agree to execute and deliver any documents, make any endorsements, and do any and all acts that may be necessary or convenient to carry out all of the terms of this agreement.

We agree that this document is intended to be the full and entire settlement and agreement between us regarding our marital rights and obligations and that this agreement should be interpreted and governed by the laws of the State of _____.

We also agree that every provision of this agreement is expressly made binding upon the heirs, assigns, executors, administrators, successors in interest, and representatives of each of us.

Signed and dated this day _____ of _____ , 19_____ .

_____   _____
[Wife's signature]   [Witness signature]

                                                        _____
                                                        [Witness signature]

_____   _____
[Husband's signature]   [Witness signature]

                                                        _____
                                                        [Witness signature]

State of _____

                              SS.

County of _____

On _____, 19 ___, _____ and _____ personally came before me and, being duly sworn, did state that they are the persons described in the above document and that they signed the above document in my presence as a free and voluntary act for the purposes stated .

_____
(Notary signature)

Notary Public, for the County of _____
State of _____
My Commission expires _____

Financial Statement

The following Financial Statement will be your record of the disclosures that you and your spouse have made to each other regarding your joint and individual economic situations. It details both your monthly income and expenses and your overall net worth (assets and liabilities). The information which you include on this form should be current and should be based upon your economic situation immediately *after* your settlement agreement takes effect. The monthly income that you list should be based on your current job and sources of income. The expenses that you include on this statement should be based on your estimated or actual expenses while you are living separate from your spouse. The assets and liabilities listed should be your separate and marital property and bills as you and your spouse have agreed to in your marital settlement agreement. Fill in only those items that apply to your circumstances.

The Financial Statement of each of you will become a permanent part of your marital settlement agreement. Both you and your spouse will need to prepare an individual copy of this statement. This form assures that both you and your spouse are fully aware of each others economic circumstances and that you have made your decisions and agreements based on full knowledge of all of the facts relating to your property and income.

Once you have both filled in the appropriate blanks on this form, re-type the entire document on clean white letter-sized paper. Then sign the document before a notary public and attach both Financial Statements to your Marital Settlement Agreement.

FINANCIAL STATEMENT OF _____

EMPLOYMENT:

Occupation: _____

Employed by:_____

Address of Employer:_____

Pay period:_____

Next pay day:_____

Rate of pay: . . . .$_____

AVERAGE MONTHLY INCOME

Gross monthly salary or wages . . . . $_____

    minus Social Security . . . . $_____

    minus income tax . . . . $_____

Other deductions from paycheck on monthly basis

    Insurance . . . .$_____

    Credit Union . . . .$_____

    Union dues . . . .$_____

    Other . . . . $_____

Net monthly salary, wages . . . . $_____

Monthly income from other sources

    Commissions, bonuses, etc. . . . . $_____

    Unemployment, welfare, etc. . . . . $_____

    Dividends, interest, etc. $_____

    Business income . . . . $_____

    Rents, royalties . . . . $_____

    Other monthly income . . . . $_____

TOTAL AVERAGE MONTHLY INCOME: . . . . $_____

AVERAGE MONTHLY EXPENSES

Mortgage or rental payment . . . . $_____

Property taxes . . . . $_____

Homeowner's insurance . . . . $_____

Electricity . . . . $_____

Water, garbage, sewer . . . . $_____

Cable television . . . . $_____

Telephone . . . . $_____

Fuel oil and natural gas . . . . $_____

Cleaning and laundry . . . . $_____

Repairs and maintenance . . . . $_____

Pest control . . . . $_____

Housewares . . . . $_____

Food and grocery items . . . . $_____

Meals outside home . . . . $_____

Clothing . . . . $_____

Medical, dental, prescriptions . . . . $_____

Education . . . . $_____

Day care/baby sitter . . . . $_____

Entertainment . . . . $_____

Gifts or donations . . . . $_____

Vacation expenses . . . . $_____

Public transportation . . . . $_____

Automobile:

      Gasoline and oil . . . . $_____

      Repairs . . . . $_____

      License . . . . $_____

      Insurance . . . . $_____

      Payments . . . . $_____

Insurance:

      Health . . . . $_____

      Disability . . . . $_____

Life . . . . $_____

Other . . . . $_____

Any other expenses (list)_____ $_____

_____ $_____

_____ $_____

Fixed debts on a monthly basis:

Creditor _____ Monthly payment $_____

Creditor _____ Monthly payment $_____

Creditor _____ Monthly payment $_____

Creditor _____ Monthly payment $_____

Any other debts:

Creditor _____ Monthly payment $_____

Creditor _____ Monthly payment $_____

Creditor _____ Monthly payment $_____

Creditor _____ Monthly payment $_____

TOTAL AVERAGE MONTHLY EXPENSES: . . . . $_____

ASSETS:

Cash: . . . . $_____

Stocks: . . . .$_____

Bonds: . . . .$_____

Real estate: . . . . $_____

Automobiles: . . . .$_____

Contents of home or apartment: . . . . $_____

Jewelry: . . . . $_____

Other: (list) _____ $_____

_____ $_____

_____ $_____

TOTAL ASSETS: . . . .$_____

LIABILITIES:

    Creditor _____ Balance due: $_____

    Creditor _____ Balance due: $_____

    Creditor _____ Balance due: $_____

    Creditor _____ Balance due: $_____

    Creditor _____ Balance due: $_____

    Creditor _____ Balance due: $_____

    Creditor _____ Balance due: $_____

    TOTAL LIABILITIES: . . . .$_____

SUMMARY OF INCOME AND EXPENSES:

    Average Monthly Income: . . . .$_____

    Average Monthly Expenses: . . . .$_____

SUMMARY OF ASSETS AND LIABILITIES:

    Total Assets: . . . .$_____

    Total Liabilities . . . .$_____

Dated this _____ day of _____, 19 _____.

_____
     [Signature]

State of _____)

SS.

County of _____)

On this day, before me, the undersigned authority, in and for and residing in the above county and state, personally appeared _____

who is personally known to me to be the same person whose name is subscribed to the foregoing document, and, being duly sworn, verified that the information contained in the foregoing document is true and correct on personal knowledge and acknowledged that said document was signed as a free and voluntary act.

Subscribed and sworn to before me this day of _____, 19 _____.

_____
[Signature of Notary Public]

Notary Public, for the County of _____

State of _____

My commission expires _____

CHAPTER 10

RELEASES

Releases are a method of acknowledging the satisfaction of an obligation or of releasing parties from liability or claims. Releases are used in various situations: from releasing a person or company from liability after an accident to a release of liens or claims against property. They can be a useful means of settling minor disputes. One party may pay another to release a claim. For example: A pays B $200.00 to release its claims for damages incurred when A's truck damaged B's garage.

Releases can be very powerful documents. The various releases contained in this chapter are tailored to meet the most common situations in which a release is used. For a release to be valid, there must be some type of consideration received by the person who is granting the release. Releases should be used carefully as they may prevent any future claims against the party to whom it is granted. In general, a release from claims relating to an accident which causes personal injury should not be signed without a prior examination by a doctor. Also note that a release relating to damage to community property in a "community property" state must be signed by both spouses. Study the various forms provided to determine which one is proper for the use intended. Please note that Chapter 16 contains a Release of Security Interest and a Release of U.C.C. Financing Statement and Chapter 17 contains a Release of Promissory Note. Please refer to those chapter for explanations of those particular release forms. The following releases are included in this chapter:

General Release: This release serves as a full blanket release from one party to another. It should only be used when all obligations of one party are to be released. The party signing this release is discharging the other party from all of their obligations to the other party stemming from a specific incident or transaction. This form can be used when one party has a claim against another and the other agrees to waive the claim for payment.

Mutual Release: The mutual release form provides a method for two parties to jointly release each other from their mutual obligations or claims. This form should be used when both parties intend to discharge each other from all of their mutual obligations. It essentially serves the purpose of two reciprocal General Releases.

Specific Release: This release form should be used when only a particular claim or obligation is being released, while allowing other liabilities to continue. The obligation being released should be spelled out in careful and precise terms to prevent confusion with any other obligation or claim. In addition, the liabilities which are not being released, but will survive, should also be carefully noted.

Release of Mechanic's Liens: This type of release will be used in the specific situation of verifying that there are no outstanding contractor's or mechanic's claims against a property for any goods or services provided in conjunction with work on the property. If there have been sub-contractors or suppliers involved in connection with the work provided, all such parties should sign this release. This release does not relieve the party to whom it is given from paying for any goods and services which have been provided. It merely releases the property itself from any potential liens by the contractors or suppliers. A complete and definite description of the property to which the release applies must be included. Since this document may be recorded, it should generally be notarized. The form provided contains a general individual acknowledgement and signature form for each of the contractors signing.

GENERAL RELEASE

For consideration, _____, residing at _____,
City of _____, State of ____, releases _____,
residing at _____, City of _____, State of _____,
from all claims and obligations, known or unknown, to this date arising from the following transaction or incident:

The party signing this release has not assigned any claims or obligations covered by this release to any other party.

The party signing this release intends that it both bind and benefit itself and any successors.

Dated: _____

_____
(Signature)

_____
(Printed name)

MUTUAL RELEASE

For consideration, _____, residing at _____
_____, City of _____, State of _____,
and _____ , residing at _____,
City of _____, State of _____, release each other from all claims
and obligations, known or unknown, to this date that they may have against each other
arising from the following transaction or incident:

Neither party has assigned any claims or obligations covered by this release to any
other party.

Both parties signing this release intend that it both bind and benefit themselves and
any successors.

_____   _____
(Signature)   (Signature)

_____   _____
(Printed name)   (Printed name)

SPECIFIC RELEASE

For consideration, _____, residing at _____,
City of _____, State of _____, releases _____
residing at _____, City of _____, State of
_____, from the following specific claims and obligations:

arising from the following transaction or incident:

Any claims or obligations that not specifically mentioned are not released by this Specific Release.

The party signing this release has not assigned any claims or obligations covered by this release to any other party.

The party signing this release intends that it both bind and benefit itself and any successors.

Dated:_____

_____
   (Signature)

_____
   (Printed name)

RELEASE OF MECHANICS LIENS

The following contractors or subcontractors have furnished materials, labor, or both for construction at the property owned by _____, and located at _____, City of _____, State of_____:

_____, _____, _____,_____
(contractor/subcontractor)   (address)   (city)   (state/zip)

_____, _____, _____,_____
(contractor/subcontractor)   (address)   (city)   (state/zip)

_____, _____, _____,_____
(contractor/subcontractor)   (address)   (city)   (state/zip)

These contractors or subcontractors hereby release all liens and the right to file any liens against this property for material or labor provided as of this date. This release does not, however, constitute a release of any sums which may be due to these contractors or subcontractors for materials or labor.

The parties signing this release intend that it both bind and benefit themselves and any successors.

Dated:_____

_____
(Contractor signature)

_____
(Contractor signature)

_____
(Contractor signature)

State of _____

County of _____

On _____, 19 __, _____ personally came before me and, being duly sworn, did state that he/she is the person described in the above document and that he/she signed the above document in my presence.

_____
(Notary signature)

Notary Public, for the County of _____

State of _____

My commission expires: _____

State of _____

County of _____

On _____, 19 __, _____ personally came before me and, being duly sworn, did state that he/she is the person described in the above document and that he/she signed the above document in my presence.

_____
(Notary signature)

Notary Public, for the County of _____

State of _____

My commission expires: _____

State of _____

County of _____

On _____, 19 __, _____ personally came before me and, being duly sworn, did state that he/she is the person described in the above document and that he/she signed the above document in my presence.

_____
(Notary signature)

Notary Public, for the County of _____

State of _____

My commission expires: _____

CHAPTER 11

RECEIPTS

In this chapter, various receipt forms are provided. In general, receipts are a formal acknowledgement of having received something, whether it is money or property. These forms do not have to be notarized. Please note that Chapter 12 contains a Receipt for Lease Security Deposit and a Rent Receipt to be used in conjunction with leases of real estate. The following receipt forms are included in this chapter:

Receipt in Full: This form should be used as a receipt for a payment which completely pays off a debt. You will need to include the amount paid, the name of the person who paid it, the date when paid, and a description of the obligation which is paid off (for example: an invoice, statement, or bill of sale). The original receipt should go to the person making the payment, but a copy should be retained.

Receipt on Account: This form should be used as a receipt for a payment which does not fully pay off a debt, but, rather, is a payment on account and is credited to the total balance due. You will need to include the amount paid, the name of the person who paid it, the date when paid, and a description of the account to which the payment is to be applied. The original receipt should go to the person making the payment, but a copy should be retained.

Receipt for Goods: This form should be used as a receipt for the acceptance of goods. It is intended to be used in conjunction with a delivery order or purchase order. It also states that the goods have been inspected and found to be in conformance with the order. The original of this receipt should be retained by the person delivering the goods and a copy should go to the person accepting delivery.

RECEIPT IN FULL

The undersigned acknowledges receipt of the sum of $ _____ paid by _____. This payment constitutes full payment and satisfaction of the following obligation:

Dated: _____

_____
(Signature of person receiving payment)

RECEIPT ON ACCOUNT

The undersigned acknowledges receipt of the sum of $_____ paid by _____. This payment will be applied and credited to the following account:

Dated: _____

_____
(Signature of person receiving payment)

RECEIPT FOR GOODS

The undersigned acknowledges receipt of the goods which are described on the attached purchase order. The undersigned also acknowledges that these goods have been inspected and found to be in conformance with the purchase order specifications.

Dated: _____

_____
(Signature of person receiving goods)

CHAPTER 12

LEASES OF REAL ESTATE

A *lease* of real estate is simply a written contract for one party to rent a specific property from another for a certain amount and for a certain time period. As such, all of the general legal ramifications that relate to contracts also relate to leases. However, all states have additional requirements which pertain only to leases. If the rental period is to be for one year or more, most states require that leases be in writing. Leases can be prepared for periodic tenancies (that is, for example, month-to-month or week-to-week) or they can be for a fixed period. The lease contained in this chapter provides for a fixed-period tenancy.

There are also general guidelines for security deposits in most states. These most often follow a reasonable pattern and should be adhered to. Most states provide for the following with regard to lease security deposits:

- Security deposits should be no greater than one month's rent and should be fully refundable;
- Security deposits should be used for the repair of damages only, and not applied for the non-payment of rent (an additional month's rent may be requested to cover potential non-payment of rent situations);
- Security deposits should be kept in a separate, interest-bearing account, and returned, with interest, to the tenant within 10 days of termination of a lease (minus, of course, any deductions for damages).

In addition to state laws regarding security deposits, many states have requirements relating to the time periods required prior to terminating a lease. These rules have evolved over time to prevent both the landlord or the tenant from being harmed by early termination of a lease. In general, if the lease is for a fixed time period, the termination of the lease is governed by the lease itself. Early termination of a fixed-period lease may, however, be governed by individual state law. For periodic leases (month-to month, etc.), there are normally state rules as to how much advance notice must be given prior to the termination of a lease. If early lease termination is anticipated, state law regarding this issue should be checked.

The following forms are included in this chapter:

Residential Lease: This form should be used when renting a residential property. The following information will be necessary to prepare this form:

- The name and address of the landlord;
- The name and address of the tenant;
- A complete legal description of the leased property;
- The length of time the lease will be in effect;
- The amount of the rental payments;
- The date of the month when the rent will be due;
- The due date of the first rent payment;
- The amount of damages security deposit;
- The amount of additional rent held as rental default deposit;
- Any utilities that the landlord will supply;
- The utilities that the tenant will provide;
- Any other additional terms (for example: no pets).

Although the landlord and tenant can agree to any terms they desire, this particular lease provides for the following basic terms to be included:

- A fixed period term for the lease;
- A security deposit for damages, which will be returned within 10 days after the termination of the lease;
- An additional month's rent as security for payment of the rent, which will be returned within 10 days after the termination of the lease;
- That the tenant agrees to keep the property in good repair and not make any alterations without consent;
- That the tenant agrees not to assign the lease or sublet the property with out the landlord's consent;
- That the landlord has the right to inspect the property on a reasonable basis, and that the tenant has already inspected it and found it satisfactory;
- That the landlord has the right to re-enter and take possession upon breach of the lease (as long as it is in accordance with state law);
- Any other additional terms that the parties agree upon.

Assignment of Lease: This form is for use if one party to a lease is assigning its full interest in the lease to another party. This effectively substitutes one party for another under a lease. This particular assignment form has both of the parties agreeing to indemnify and hold each other harmless for any failures to perform under the lease while they were the party liable under it. This *indemnify and hold harmless* clause simply means that if a claim arises for failure to perform each party agrees to be responsible for the period of their own performance obligations. A description of the lease which is assigned should include the parties to the lease, a description of the property, and the date of the lease. Other information that is necessary to complete the assignment is the name and address of the *assignor* (the party who is assigning the lease), the name and address of the *assignee* (the party to whom the lease is being assigned), and the date of the assignment. A copy of the original lease should be attached to this form. A copy of a Consent to Assignment of Lease should also be attached, if necessary.

Consent to Assignment of Lease: This form is used if the original lease states that the consent of the landlord is necessary for the assignment of the lease to be valid. A description of the lease and the name and signature of the person giving the consent are all that is necessary for completing this form. A copy of the original lease should be attached to this form.

Notice of Assignment of Lease: If a third party is involved in any of the obligations or benefits of an assigned lease, that party should be notified of the assignment in writing. This alerts the third party to look to the new party for satisfaction of any obligations under the lease or to make any payments under the lease directly to the new party. Information necessary to complete this form is the names and addresses of the parties to the lease, a description of the lease, and the effective date of the assignment of the lease. A copy of the original lease should be attached to this form. A copy of a Consent to Assignment of Lease should also be attached, if necessary.

Amendment of Lease: Use this form to modify any terms of a lease (other than the expiration date: see below). It may be used to change any portion of the lease. Simply note what changes are being made in the appropriate place on this form. If a portion of the lease is being deleted, make note of the deletion. If certain language is being substituted, state the substitution clearly. If additional language is being added, make this clear. A copy of the original lease should be attached to this form. For example, you may wish to use language as follows:

- "Paragraph _____ is deleted from this lease.:
- "Paragraph _____ is deleted from this lease and the following paragraph is substituted in its place:"
- "The following new paragraph is added to this lease:"

150

Extension of Lease: This document should be used to extend the effective time period during which a lease is in force. The use of this form allows the time limit to be extended without having to entirely re-draft the lease. Under this document, all of the other terms of the lease will remain the same, with only the expiration date changing. You will need to fill in the original expiration date and the new expiration date. Other information necessary will be the names and addresses of the parties to the lease and a description of the lease. A copy of the original lease should be attached to this form.

Sublease: This form is used if the tenant subleases the property covered by an original lease. This particular sublease form has both of the parties agreeing to indemnify and hold each other harmless for any failures to perform under the lease while they were the party liable under it. This *indemnify and hold harmless* clause simply means that if a claim arises for failure to perform each party agrees to be responsible for the period of their own performance obligations. A description of the lease which is subleased should include the parties to the lease, a description of the property, and the date of the lease. Other information that is necessary to complete the sublease is the name and address of the original tenant, the name and address of the *sub-tenant* (the party to whom the property is being subleased), and the date of the sublease. A copy of the original lease should be attached to this form. A copy of a Consent to Sublease of Lease should also be attached, if necessary.

Consent to Sublease: This form is used if the original lease states that the consent of the landlord is necessary for a sublease to be valid. A description of the lease and the name and signature of the person giving the consent are all that is necessary for completing this form. A copy of the original lease should be attached to this form.

Notice of Breach of Lease: This form should be used to notify a party to a lease of the violation of a term of the lease or of an instance of failure to perform a required duty under the lease. It provides for a description of the alleged violation of the lease and for a time period in which the party is instructed to cure the breach of the lease. If the breach is not taken care of within the time period allowed, a lawyer should be consulted for further action, which may entail a lawsuit to enforce the lease terms. A copy of the original lease should be attached to this form.

Notice of Rent Default: This form allows for notice to a tenant of default in the payment of rent. It provides for the amount of the defaulted payments to be specified and for a time limit to be placed on payment before further action is taken. If the breach is not taken care of within the time period allowed, a lawyer should be consulted for further action, which may involve a lawsuit to enforce the lease terms. A copy of the original lease should be attached to this form.

Notice to Vacate Property: This notice informs a tenant who has already been notified of a breach of the lease (or of a late rent payment) to vacate the property. It sets a specific date by which the tenant must be out of the property. If the tenant fails to leave by the date set, an attorney should be consulted to begin eviction efforts.

Landlord's Notice to Terminate Lease: By this notice, a landlord may inform a tenant of the unilateral termination of a lease for breach of the lease. This action may be taken under the leases provided in this book because there are specific lease provisions that allow this action and (presumably) the tenant has agreed to these provisions. To complete this form, the lease should be described; the breach of the lease should be described; the date of the original Breach of Lease notice should be noted; and a date on which the tenant should deliver possession of the property to the landlord should be set.

Tenant's Notice to Terminate Lease: By this notice, a tenant may inform a landlord of the unilateral termination of a lease for breach of the lease. This action may be taken under the leases provided in this book because there are specific lease provisions that allow this action and (presumably) the landlord has agreed to these provisions. To complete this form, the lease should be described; the breach of the lease (reason for termination) should be described; and the date for delivery of possession back to the landlord should be set.

Mutual Termination of Lease: This form should be used when both the landlord and tenant desire to terminate a lease. To complete, simply fill in the names of the landlord and tenant and a description of the lease. This document releases both parties from any claims that the other may have against them for any actions under the lease. It also states that the landlord agrees that the rent has been paid in full and that the property has been delivered in good condition.

Receipt for Lease Security Deposit: This form is to be used for receipt of a lease security deposit. The amount of the deposit and a description of the leased property are all that is necessary for completion.

Rent Receipt: This form may be used as a receipt for the periodic payment of rent. It provides for the amount paid; the period paid for; and a description of the property.

Notice of Lease: This document should be used to record notice that a parcel of real estate has a current lease in effect on it. This may be necessary if the property is on the market for sale or it may be required by a bank or mortgage company. Requiring a notarization, this form may be completed with the following information: name and address of the landlord and tenant; description of the property; term of the lease and any options to extend.

RESIDENTIAL LEASE

This Lease is made on _____, 19 ___, between _____

_____, Landlord, residing at _____, City of _____,

State of _____, and _____, Tenant, residing at _____,

City of _____, State of _____.

1.   The Landlord agrees to rent to the Tenant and the Tenant agrees to rent from the Landlord the following residence:

2.   The term of this lease will be from _____ , 19 ___, until

_____, 19 ___.

3.   The rental payments will be $_____ per _____ and will be payable by the Tenant to the Landlord on the _____ day of each month, beginning on _____, 19 ___.

4.   The Tenant has paid the Landlord a security deposit of $ _____. This security deposit will be held as security for the repair of any damages to the residence by the Tenant. This deposit will be returned to the Tenant within 10 days of the termination of this lease, minus any amounts needed to repair the residence.

5.   The Tenant has paid the Landlord an additional month's rent in the amount of $ _____. This rent deposit will be held as security for the payment of rent by the Tenant. This rent payment deposit will be returned to the Tenant within 10 days of the termination of this lease, minus any rent still due upon termination.

6.   Tenant agrees to maintain the residence in a clean and sanitary manner and not to make any alterations to the residence without the Landlord's written consent. Tenant also agrees not to conduct any business in the residence. At the termination of this lease, the Tenant agrees to leave the residence in the same condition as when it was received, except for normal wear and tear.

7. The Landlord agrees to supply the following utilities to the Tenant:

8. The Tenant agrees to obtain and pay for the following utilities:

9. Tenant agrees not to sub-let the residence or assign this lease without the Landlord's written consent. Tenant agrees to allow the Landlord reasonable access to the residence for inspection and repair. Landlord agrees to only enter the residence after notifying the Tenant in advance, except in an emergency.

10. The Tenant has inspected the residence and has found it satisfactory.

11. If the Tenant fails to pay the rent on time or violates any other terms of this lease, the Landlord will have the right to terminate this lease in accordance with state law. The Landlord will also have the right to re-enter the residence and take possession of it and to take advantage of any other legal remedies available.

12. The following are additional terms of this Lease:

13. The parties agree that this lease is the entire agreement between them. This Lease binds and benefits both the Landlord and Tenant and any successors.

_____   _____
(Signature of landlord)   *(Signature of tenant)*

_____   _____
(Printed name of landlord)   *(Printed name of tenant)*

ASSIGNMENT OF LEASE

This Assignment is made on _____, 19 __, between _____

_____, Assignor, residing at _____, City of_____

_____, State of _____, and _____, Assignee,

residing at _____ , City of _____, State of _____.

For valuable consideration, the parties agree to the following terms and conditions:

1.   The Assignor assigns all interest, burdens, and benefits in the following described lease to the Assignee:
This lease is attached to this Assignment and is a part of this Assignment.

2.   The Assignor warrants that this lease is in effect, has not been modified, and is
fully assignable. If the consent of the Landlord is necessary for this Assignment to be
effective, such consent is attached to this Assignment and is a part of this Assignment.
Assignor agrees to indemnify and hold the Assignee harmless from any claim which
may result from the Assignor's failure to perform under this lease prior to the date of
this Assignment.

3.   The Assignee agrees to perform all of the obligations of the Assignor and receive all of the benefits of the Assignor under this lease. Assignee agrees to indemnify
and hold the Assignor harmless from any claim which may result from the Assignee's
failure to perform under this lease after the date of this Assignment.

4.   This Assignment binds and benefits both parties and any successors. This document, including any attachments, is the entire agreement between the parties.

_____   _____
(Signature of Assignor)   *(Signature of Assignee)*

_____   _____
(Printed name of Assignor)   *(Printed name of Assignee)*

CONSENT TO ASSIGNMENT OF LEASE

Date: _____

To:

1.   I am the Landlord under the following described Lease:

This Lease is the subject of the attached Assignment of Lease.

I consent to the Assignment of this Lease as described in the attached Assignment, which provides that the Assignee is fully substituted for the Assignor.

_____
(Signature of landlord)

_____
(name of landlord)

NOTICE OF ASSIGNMENT OF LEASE

Date: _____

To:

RE: Assignment of Lease

Dear _____:

This notice is in reference to the following described lease:

Please be advised that as of _____, 19 ___, all interest and rights under this lease which were formerly owned by _____,
residing at _____, City of _____, State of _____,
have been permanently assigned to _____,
residing at _____, City of _____, State of _____,

Please be advised that all of the obligations and rights of the former party to this lease
are now the responsibility of the new party to this lease.

_____
(Signature)

_____
(Printed name)

AMENDMENT OF LEASE

This Amendment of Lease is made on _____, 19 ___, between _____, residing at _____, City of_____ State of _____, and _____, residing at _____, City of _____, State of _____.

For valuable consideration, the parties agree as follows:

1.   The following described lease is attached to this Amendment and is made a part of this Amendment:

2.   The parties agree to amend this lease as follows:

3.   All other terms and conditions of the original lease remain in effect without modification. This Amendment binds and benefits both parties and any successors. This document, including the attached lease, is the entire agreement between the parties.

The parties have signed this amendment on the date specified at the beginning of this Amendment.

_____
(Signature of landlord)

_____
(Signature of tenant)

_____
(Printed name of landlord)

_____
(Printed name of tenant)

EXTENSION OF LEASE

This Extension of Lease is made on _____, 19 ___, between
_____, residing at _____, City of _____,
State of _____, and _____, residing at _____,
City of _____, State of _____.

For valuable consideration, the parties agree as follows:

1.   The following described lease will end on _____, 19 ___:

This lease is attached to this Extension and is a part of this Extension.

2.   The parties agree to extend this lease for an additional period, which will
begin immediately on the expiration of the original time period and will end on
_____, 19 ___.

3.   The Extension of this lease will be on the same terms and conditions as the
original lease. This Extension binds and benefits both parties and any successors. This
document, including the attached lease, is the entire agreement between the parties.

The parties have signed this Extension on the date specified at the beginning of this
Extension.

_____   _____
(Signature of landlord)   *(Signature of tenant)*

_____   _____
(Printed name of landlord)   *(Printed name of tenant)*

SUBLEASE

This Sublease is made on _____, 19 ___, between _____
_____, Tenant, residing at _____, City of_____
_____, State of _____, and _____, Sub-tenant,
residing at _____ , City of _____, State of _____.

For valuable consideration, the parties agree to the following terms and conditions:

1. The Tenant subleases to the Sub-tenant the following described property:

2.   This property is currently leased to the Tenant under the terms of the following
described lease:

This lease is attached to this Sublease and is a part of this Sublease.

3.   This Sublease will be for the period from _____, 19 ___, to
_____, 19 ___.

4.   The sub-rental payments will be $_____ per _____ and will be
payable by the Subtenant to the Landlord on the _____ day of each month,
beginning on _____, 19 ___.

5.   The Tenant warrants that the underlying lease is in effect, has not been modified, and that the property may be sublet. If the consent of the Landlord is necessary for his Sublease to be effective, such consent is attached to this Sublease and is a part of this Sublease. Tenant agrees to indemnify and hold the Sub-tenant harmless from any claim which may result from the Tenant's failure to perform under this lease prior to the date of this Sublease.

6.   The Sub-tenant agrees to perform all of the obligations of the Tenant under the original lease and receive all of the benefits of the Tenant under this lease. Sub-tenant agrees to indemnify and hold the Tenant harmless from any claim which may result from the Sub-tenant's failure to perform under this lease after the date of this Sublease.

7.   The Tenant agrees to remain primarily liable to the Landlord for the obligations under the Lease.

8.   The parties agree to the following additional terms:

9.   This Sublease binds and benefits both parties and any successors. This document, including any attachments, is the entire agreement between the parties.

_____   _____
(Signature of tenant)   *(Signature of sub-tenant)*

_____   _____
(Printed name of tenant)   *(Printed name of sub-tenant)*

CONSENT TO SUBLEASE

Date: _____

To:

1.   I am the Landlord under the following described Lease:

This Lease is the subject of the attached Sublease.

I consent to the Sublease of this Lease as described in the attached Sublease, which provides that the Sub-tenant is substituted for the Tenant for the period indicated in the Sublease. This consent does not release the Tenant from any obligations under the lease and the Tenant remains fully bound under the Lease.

_____
(Signature of landlord)

_____
(Printed name of landlord)

NOTICE OF BREACH OF LEASE

Date: _____

To:

RE: Breach of Lease

Dear _____:

This notice is in reference to the following described lease:

Please be advised that as of _____, 19 ___, we are holding you in BREACH OF LEASE for the following reasons:

If this breach of lease is not corrected within _____ days of this notice, we will take further action to protect our rights, which may include termination of this lease. This notice is made under all applicable laws. All of our rights are reserved under this notice.

_____
(Signature of landlord)

_____
(Printed name of landlord)

NOTICE OF RENT DEFAULT

Date: _____

To:

RE: Notice of Rent Default

Dear _____:

This notice is in reference to the following described lease:

Please be advised that as of _____, 19 ___, you are in DEFAULT IN YOUR PAYMENT OF RENT in the amount of $ _____.

If this breach of lease is not corrected within _____ days of this notice, we will take further action to protect our rights, which may include termination of this lease and collection proceedings. This notice is made under all applicable laws. All of our rights are reserved under this notice.

_____
(Signature of landlord)

_____
(Printed name of landlord)

NOTICE TO VACATE PROPERTY

Date: _____

To:

RE: Notice to Vacate Property

Dear _____:

This notice is in reference to the following described lease:

Please be advised that since _____, 19 ___, you have been in BREACH OF LEASE for the following reasons:

You were previously notified of this breach in the NOTICE dated _____ _____, 19 ___. At that time you were given _____ days to correct the breach of the lease and you have not complied.

THEREFORE, YOU ARE HEREBY GIVEN NOTICE:

To immediately vacate the property and deliver possession to the Landlord on or before _____, 19 ___. If you fail to correct the breach of lease or vacate the property by this date, legal action to evict you from the property will be taken. Regardless of your vacating the property, you are still responsible for all rent due under the lease.

_____
(Signature of landlord)

_____
(Printed name of landlord)

LANDLORD'S NOTICE TO TERMINATE LEASE

Date: _____

To:

RE: Notice to Terminate Lease

Dear _____:

This notice is in reference to the following described lease:

Please be advised that as of _____, 19 ___, you have been in
BREACH OF LEASE for the following reasons:

You were previously notified of this breach in the NOTICE dated _____
_____, 19 ___. At that time you were given _____ days to correct the breach
of the lease and you have not complied.

THEREFORE, YOU ARE HEREBY GIVEN NOTICE:

The lease is immediately terminated and you are directed to deliver possession of the
property to the Landlord on or before _____, 19 ___. If you fail to deliver the property by this date, legal action to evict you from the property will be
taken. Regardless of your deliverance of the property, you are still responsible for all
rent due under the lease.

_____
(Signature of landlord)

_____
(Printed name of landlord)

TENANT'S NOTICE TO TERMINATE LEASE

Date: _____

To:

RE: Notice to Terminate Property

Dear _____:

This notice is in reference to the following described lease:

Please be advised that as of _____, 19 ___, we are terminating the lease for the following reasons:

We intend to deliver possession of the property to the Landlord on or before _____, 19 ___.

_____
(Signature of tenant)

_____
(Printed name of tenant)

MUTUAL TERMINATION OF LEASE

This Termination of Lease is made on _____, 19 ___, between
_____, residing at _____, City of _____,
State of _____, and _____, residing at _____,
City of _____, State of _____.

For valuable consideration, the parties agree as follows:

1.   The parties are currently bound under the terms of the following described lease:

2.   They agree to mutually terminate and cancel this lease effective on this date. This Termination Agreement will act as a mutual release of all obligations under this lease for both parties, as if the lease has not been entered into in the first place. Landlord agrees that all rent due has been paid and that the possession of the property has been returned in satisfactory condition.

3.   This Termination binds and benefits both parties and any successors. This document, including the attached lease being terminated, is the entire agreement between the parties.

The parties have signed this Termination on the date specified at the beginning of this Termination.

_____
(Signature of landlord)

_____
(Signature of tenant)

_____
(Printed name of landlord)

_____
(Printed name of tenant)

RECEIPT FOR LEASE SECURITY DEPOSIT

The Landlord acknowledges receipt of the sum of $_____ paid by the Tenant under the following described lease:

This Security Deposit payment will be held by the Landlord under the terms of this lease, and unless required by law, will not bear any interest. This Security Deposit will be repaid when due under the terms of the lease.

Dated: _____

_____
(Signature of landlord)

_____
(Printed name of landlord)

RENT RECEIPT

The Landlord acknowledges receipt of the sum of $_____ paid by _____. This payment will be applied and credited to the rent due for the period of _____, 19 ___, on the following described property:

Dated: _____

_____
(Signature of landlord)

_____
(Printed name of landlord)

NOTICE OF LEASE

NOTICE is given of the existence of the following lease:

Name and Address of Landlord:

Name and Address of Tenant:

Description of property leased:

Term of lease: From _____, 19 ___, to _____ 19 ___.

Any options to extend lease:

_____
(Signature)

_____
(Printed name)

State of _____
County of _____

On _____, 19 ___, _____ personally came before me and, being duly sworn, did state that he/she is the person described in the above document and that he/she signed the above document in my presence.

_____
(Notary signature)

Notary Public, for the County of _____
State of _____
My commission expires: _____

CHAPTER 13

RENTAL OF PERSONAL PROPERTY

Leases of personal property are often undertaken in the context of tools, equipment, or property necessary to perform a certain task. Other situations where such an agreement is often used is in the rental of property for recreational purposes. The needs of the parties to a personal property rental agreement depend a great deal on the type of property involved and the value of the property.

The two basic forms that are included in this chapter are somewhat at both ends of the spectrum with regard to rental of personal property. The first form is a very simple rental agreement that can be used for short-term rentals of relatively inexpensive property. The second form is a much more complex form that may be used for rentals of more valuable property. A personally-tailored form may be constructed by adding particular clauses from the second form to the first form as the circumstances of a particular business situation dictate. Two termination of rental agreement forms are also included.

Personal Property Rental Agreement (Simple): This form is designed to be used in situations involving inexpensive property for short terms. As you will see by comparing these clauses to those present in the next form, this form does not address many of the potential problems that may arise in the rental of personal property. However, it does provide a legal basis for an enforceable contract between two parties regarding the rental of personal property.

The information necessary for the preparation of this form is simply the names and addresses of the parties (the *owner* and the *renter*); a description of the property; and the amount and term of the rental.

Personal Property Rental Agreement (Complex): This particular form is a far more detailed version of the basic rental agreement described above. It is designed to be used in situations that call for more attention to potential problems relating to the rental. This generally means situations in which the property is more valuable.

This agreement addresses the following areas of concern:

- The inspection of the property by the renter and the renter's agreement to use the property in a careful manner;
- A warranty by the owner that the property is safe and in good condition;
- An indemnity agreement by the renter for damage to the property;
- A disclaimer of liability by the owner;
- Provisions for a security deposit to cover damages or late rental payments;
- An agreement by the renter not to assign or transfer the property;
- Responsibility for insuring the property;
- Provisions for mediation and arbitration of disputes:

The information necessary for filling in this form is as follows:

- The names and addresses of the parties (the owner and the renter);
- A description of the property;
- The amount and term of the rental;
- The amount of insurance to be provided by the renter;
- Any additional terms the parties desire.

Renter's Notice to Terminate Rental Agreement: This form is to be used by the renter to provide the written notice required to terminate the complex personal property rental agreement. Simply fill in the name of the renter and owner; a description of the rental agreement; and the date and reason for the termination.

Owner's Notice to Terminate Rental Agreement: This form is essentially identical to the above form, but is designed to be used by the owner (rather than the renter) to terminate the agreement. Fill in the name of the renter and owner; a description of the rental agreement; and the date and reason for the termination.

PERSONAL PROPERTY RENTAL AGREEMENT
(Simple)

This Agreement is made on _____, 19 ___, between _____
_____, Owner, residing at _____, City of _____,
State of _____, and _____, Renter, residing at _____,
City of _____, State of _____.

1.   The Owner agrees to rent to the Renter and the Renter agrees to rent from the Owner the following property:

2.   The term of this Agreement will be from ___ o'clock _____ m. _____
19 ___, until _____ o'clock _____ m., _____, 19 ___.

3.   The rental payments will be $_____ per _____ and will be payable by the Renter to the Owner as follows:

4.   This Agreement may be terminated by either party by giving 24 hours notice to the other party.

5.   The parties agree that this Agreement is the entire agreement between them. This Agreement binds and benefits both the Owner and Renter and any successors.

_____   _____
(Signature of Owner)   *(Signature of Renter)*

_____   _____
(name of Owner)   *(name of Renter)*

PERSONAL PROPERTY RENTAL AGREEMENT
(Complex)

This Agreement is made on _____, 19 ___, between _____ _____, Owner, residing at _____, City of _____, State of _____, and _____, Renter, residing at _____, City of _____, State of _____.

1.   The Owner agrees to rent to the Renter and the Renter agrees to rent from the Owner the following property:

2.   The term of this Agreement will be from ___ o'clock _____ m. _____ 19 ___, until _____ o'clock _____ m., _____, 19 ___.

3.   The rental payments will be $_____ per _____ and will be payable by the Renter to the Owner as follows:

4.   The Renter agrees to pay a late fee of $_____ per day that the rental payment is late. If the rental payments are in default for over _____ days, the Owner may immediately demand possession of the property without advance notice to the Renter.

5.   The Owner warrants that the property is free of any known faults which would affect its safe operation under normal usage and is in good working condition. The Renter states that the property has been inspected and is in good working condition. The Renter agrees to use the property in a safe manner and in normal usage and to maintain the property in good repair. The Renter further agrees not to use the property in a negligent manner or for any illegal purpose.

7.   The Renter agrees to fully indemnify the Owner for any damage to or loss of the property during the term of this Agreement, unless such loss or damage is caused by a defect of the rented property. The Owner shall not be liable for any injury, loss, or damage caused by any use of the property.

9.   The Renter has paid the Owner a security deposit of $ _____. This security deposit will be held as security for payments of the rent and for the repair of any damages to the property by the Renter. This deposit will be returned to the Renter upon the termination of this Agreement, minus any rent still owed to the Owner and minus any amounts needed to repair the property, beyond normal wear and tear.

10.   The Renter may not assign or transfer any rights under this Agreement to any other person, nor allow the property to be used by any other person, without the written consent of the Owner.

11.   Renter agrees to obtain insurance coverage for the property during the term of this rental agreement in the amount of $ _____. Renter agrees to provide the Owner with a copy of the insurance policy and to not cancel the policy during the term of this rental agreement.

12.__This Agreement may be terminated by either party by giving 24 hours written notice to the other party. Any dispute related to this agreement will be settled by voluntary mediation. If mediation is unsuccessful, the dispute will be settled by binding arbitration using an arbitrator of the American Arbitration Association. The parties agree that this Agreement is the entire agreement between them. This Agreement binds and benefits both the Owner and Renter and any successors. Time is of the essence of this Agreement. This Agreement is governed by the laws of the State of _____.

13.   The following are additional terms of this Agreement:

_____   _____
(Signature of owner)   *(Signature of renter)*

_____   _____
(Name of owner)   *(Name of renter)*

RENTER'S NOTICE TO TERMINATE RENTAL AGREEMENT

Date: _____

To:

RE: Notice to Terminate Rental Agreement

Dear _____:

This notice is in reference to the following described Personal Property Rental Agreement:

Please be advised that as of _____, 19 ___, we are terminating the Personal Property Rental Agreement for the following reasons:

We intend to deliver possession of the property to the Owner on or before _____, 19 ___.

_____
(Signature of renter)

_____
(name of renter)

OWNER'S NOTICE TO TERMINATE RENTAL AGREEMENT

Date: _____

To:

RE: Notice to Terminate Rental Agreement

Dear _____:

This notice is in reference to the following described Personal Property Rental Agreement:

Please be advised that as of _____, 19 ___, we are terminating the Personal Property Rental Agreement for the following reasons:

Please deliver possession of the property to the Owner on or before _____, 19 ___.

_____
(Signature of owner)

_____
(Name of owner)

CHAPTER 14

SALE OF PERSONAL PROPERTY

The forms in this chapter are for use when selling personal property. A contract for the sale of personal property may be part of a greater transaction (involving, for example, the sale of real estate or a complete business) or it may be prepared separate from any other dealings. A *bill of sale* provides a receipt for both parties that the sale has been consummated and the delivery of the item in question has taken place. Bills of sale are often utilized to document the sale of personal property that is part of a real estate transaction when the terms of the sale are part of the real estate sales contract.

The following forms are provided in this section:

Contract for Sale of Personal Property: This form may be used for documenting the sale of any type of personal property. It may be used for vehicles, business assets, or any other personal property. The information necessary to complete this form is the names and addresses of the seller and the buyer; a complete description of the property being sold; the total purchase price; and the terms of the payment of this price.

Bill of Sale, with Warranties: This document is used as a receipt of the sale of personal property. It is, in many respects, often used to operate as a "title" to items of personal property. It verifies that the person noted in the bill of sale has obtained legal title to the property from the previous owner. This particular version also provides that the seller warrants that she/he has authority to transfer legal title to the buyer and that there are no outstanding debts or liabilities for the property. In addition, this form provides that the seller warrants that the property is in good working condition on the date of the sale. To complete this form, simply fill in the names and addresses of the seller and buyer; the purchase price of the item; and a description of the property.

Bill of Sale, without Warranties: This form also provides a receipt to the buyer for the purchase of an item of personal property. However, in this form, the seller makes no warranties at all, either regarding the authority to sell the item or the condition of the item. It is sold to the buyer in "as is" condition. The buyer takes it regardless of any defects. To complete this form, fill in the names and addresses of the seller and buyer; the purchase price of the item; and a description of the property.

Bill of Sale, subject to Debt: This form also provides a receipt to the buyer for the purchase of an item of personal property. This form, however, provides that the property sold is subject to a certain prior debt. It verifies that the seller has obtained legal title to the property from the previous owner, but that the seller specifies that the property is sold subject to a certain debt which the buyer is to pay off. In addition, the buyer agrees to indemnify the seller regarding any liability on the debt. This particular version also provides that the seller warrants that he or she has authority to transfer legal title to the buyer. In addition, this form provides that the owner warrants that the property is in good working condition on the date of the sale. To complete this form, fill in the names and addresses of the seller and buyer; the purchase price of the item; a description of the property; and a description of the debt.

CONTRACT FOR SALE OF PERSONAL PROPERTY

This Contract is made on _____, 19 ___, between _____ _____, Seller, residing at _____, City of _____, State of _____, and _____, Buyer, residing at _____, City of _____, State of _____.

1.   The Seller agrees to sell to the Buyer, and the Buyer agrees to buy the following personal property:

2.   The Buyer agrees to pay the Seller $_____ for the property. The Buyer agrees to pay this purchase price in the following manner:

3.   The Buyer will be entitled to possession of this property on _____, 19 _____.

4.   The Seller represents that it has legal title to the property and full authority to sell the property. Seller also represents that the property is sold free and clear of all liens, indebtedness, or liabilities. Seller agrees to provide Buyer with a Bill of Sale for the property.

5.   This Contract binds and benefits both the Buyer and Seller and any successors. This document, including any attachments, is the entire agreement between the Buyer and Seller. This Agreement is governed by the laws of the State of _____.

_____
(Signature)

_____
(Signature)

_____
(Printed name)

_____
(Printed name)

BILL OF SALE, WITH WARRANTIES

This Bill of Sale is made on _____, 19 ___, between _____ _____, Seller, residing at _____, City of _____, State of _____, and _____, Buyer, residing at _____, City of _____, State of _____.

In exchange for the payment of $ _____ , received from the Buyer, the Seller sells and transfers possession of the following property to the Buyer:

The Seller warrants that it owns this property and that it has the authority to sell the property to the Buyer. Seller also warrants that the property is sold free and clear of all liens, indebtedness, or liabilities.

The Seller also warrants that the property is in good working condition as of this date.

Signed and delivered to the Buyer on the above date.

_____
(Signature)

_____
(Printed name of seller)

BILL OF SALE, WITHOUT WARRANTIES

This Bill of Sale is made on _____, 19 ___, between _____

_____, Seller, residing at _____, City of _____,

State of _____, and _____, Buyer, residing at _____,

City of _____, State of _____.

In exchange for the payment of $ _____, received from the Buyer, the

Seller sells and transfers possession of the following property to the Buyer:

The Seller disclaims any implied warranty of merchantability or fitness and the property is sold in its present condition, "as is".

Signed and delivered to the Buyer on the above date.

_____
(Signature)

_____
(Printed name of seller)

BILL OF SALE, SUBJECT TO DEBT

This Bill of Sale is made on _____, 19 ___, between _____

_____, Seller, residing at _____, City of _____,

State of _____, and _____, Buyer, residing at _____,

City of _____, State of _____.

In exchange for the payment of $ _____ , received from the Buyer, the

Seller sells and transfers possession of the following property to the Buyer:

The Seller warrants that it owns this property and that it has the authority to sell the

property to the Buyer. Seller also states that the property is sold subject to the follow-

ing debt:

The Buyer buys the property subject to the above debt and agrees to pay the debt.

Buyer also agrees to indemnify and hold the Seller harmless from any claim based on

failure to pay off this debt.

The Seller also warrants that the property is in good working condition as of this date.

Signed and delivered to the Buyer on the above date.

_____   _____
(Signature of seller)   *(Signature of buyer)*

_____   _____
(Printed name of seller)   *(Printed name of buyer)*

CHAPTER 15

SALE OF REAL ESTATE

In this chapter are various forms for the sale and transfer of real estate. Although most real estate sales today are handled by real estate professionals, it is still perfectly legal to buy and sell property without the use of a real estate broker or lawyer. The forms provided in this chapter allow an individual to prepare the necessary forms for many basic real estate transactions. Please note, however, that there may be various state and local variations on sales contracts, mortgages, or other real estate documents. If in doubt, please check with a local real estate professional or an attorney. The following forms are provided:

Contract for Sale of Real Estate: This form may be used for setting down an agreement to buy and sell property. It contains the basic clauses to cover situations that will arise in most typical real estate transaction. The following items are covered:

- That the sale is conditioned on the buyer being able to obtain financing 30 days prior to the closing;
- That if the sale is not completed, the buyer will be given back the earnest money deposit, without interest or penalty;
- That the seller will provide a Warranty Deed for the real estate and a Bill of Sale for any personal property included in the sale;
- That certain items will be pro-rated and adjusted as of the closing date;
- That the buyer and the seller may split the various closing costs;
- That the seller represents that it has good title to the property and that the personal property included is in good working order.
- That the title to the property will be evidenced by either title insurance or an abstract of title;

In order to prepare this contract, the following information will be necessary:

- The names and addresses of the buyer and seller:
- A description of the property involved;
- The purchase price of the property;
- How the purchase price will be paid;
- The amount of earnest money paid on signing the contract;
- The date, place, and time for closing the sale;
- Which items will be adjusted and pro-rated at closing;
- Which closing costs will be paid for by the seller and which by the buyer;
- Whether there are any outstanding claims, liabilities, or indebtedness pertaining to the property;
- Whether there are any additional terms;
- Which state's laws will be used to interpret the contract.

Title insurance or an abstract of title will need to be obtained from a local title company or attorney. Finally, a Bill of Sale for any personal property (Chapter 14) and a Warranty Deed will need to be prepared for use at the closing of the sale.

Option to Buy Real Estate Agreement: This form is designed to be used to offer an interested buyer a time period in which to have an exclusive option to purchase a parcel of real estate. It should be used in conjunction with a filled-in but unsigned copy of the above Contract for the Sale of Real Estate. Through the use of this agreement, the seller can offer the buyer a time with which to consider the purchase without concern of a sale to another party.

This agreement provides that in exchange for a payment (which will be applied to the purchase price if the option is exercised), the buyer is given a period of time to accept the terms of a completed real estate contract. If the buyer accepts the terms and exercises the option in writing, the seller agrees to complete the sale. If the option is not exercised, the seller is then free to sell the property on the market and to retain the money paid for the option.

To complete this form, you will need the following information:

- The names and addresses of the buyer and seller:
- A description of the property involved;
- The amount of money to be paid for the option;
- The time limit of the option;
- The purchase price of the property.

In addition, a Contract for the Sale of Real Estate covering the property subject to the option should be completed and attached to the option agreement. This contract will provide all of the essential terms of the actual agreement to sell the property.

Quitclaim Deed: Any transfers of real estate must be in writing. This type of deed is intended to be used when the seller is merely selling whatever interest he or she may have in the property. By using a quitclaim deed, a seller is not, in any way, guaranteeing that he or she actually owns any interest in the property. This type of deed may be used to settle any claims that a person may have to a piece of real estate, to settle disputes over property, or to transfer property between co-owners.

To prepare this deed, simply fill in the names and addresses of the *grantor* (the one transferring the property) and the *grantee* (the one receiving the property) and the legal description of the property. For this deed form to be recorded, it must be properly notarized.

Warranty Deed: This type of deed is used in most real estate situations. It provides that the seller is conveying to the buyer a full and complete title to the land without any restrictions or debts. If there are restrictions or debts that the buyer will take the property subject to, these should be noted in the legal description area provided.

To complete this deed, simply fill in the names and addresses of the *grantor* (the one selling the property) and the *grantee* (the one buying the property) and the legal description of the property. For the transfer to actually take place, the grantor must give the actual deed to the grantee. In addition, in order for this document to be recorded, this form should be properly notarized.

Affidavit Of Title: This specialized type of affidavit is used in real estate transactions to verify certain information regarding a piece of property. An Affidavit of Title is often required by a mortgage lender prior to approving a mortgage. With an Affidavit of Title, a landowner or seller states, under oath, that they have full possession and ownership of the property being sold. They also state the existence of any liens or claims against the property and that they have full authority to sell the property.

The information necessary for filling in this form is the name and address of the seller of the property; a complete legal description of the property; and a description of any liens or claims against the property. This form should be notarized as it may be required to be recorded.

Deed of Trust: A deed of trust is a document that creates a security interest in a parcel of property. It is similar to a mortgage. It does not create the debt itself and so must be used in conjunction with a promissory note (from Chapter 17). Some states use *mortgages* for this purpose and some states entitle such documents *deeds of trust*. The purpose of both is the same. This document must be notarized and recorded in land records office of the county where the property is located in order to be effective. Because of the many local and state variations in these type of documents, this document is for informational purposes only. Please consult an attorney or real estate professional for information regarding preparation of a locally-acceptable deed of trust.

Mortgage: A mortgage is also a document that creates a security interest in a parcel of property, similar to a deed of trust. It does not create the debt itself and so must be used in conjunction with a promissory note (from Chapter 17). Some states use *mortgages* for this purpose and while other states refer to such documents as *deeds of trust*. The purpose of both is the same: to create a security interest in the real estate. This document must be notarized and recorded in land records office of the county where the property is located in order to be effective. Because of the many local and state variations in these type of documents, this document is provided here for informational purposes only. You are strongly advised to consult an attorney or real estate professional for information regarding preparation of a locally- acceptable mortgage.

CONTRACT FOR SALE OF REAL ESTATE

This Contract is made on _____, 19 ___, between _____ _____, Seller, residing at _____, City of _____, State of _____, and _____, Buyer, residing at _____, City of _____, State of _____.

The Seller now owns the following described real estate, located at _____ _____, City of _____, State of _____:

For valuable consideration, the Seller agrees to sell and the Buyer agrees to buy this property for the following price and on the following terms:

1.   The Seller will sell this property to the Buyer, free from all claims, liabilities, and indebtedness. The following personal property is included in this sale:

2.   The Buyer agrees to pay the Seller the sum of $ _____ , which the Seller agrees to accept as full payment. This Agreement, however, is conditional upon the Buyer being able to arrange suitable financing on the following terms at least 30 days prior to the closing date for this Agreement:

3.   The purchase price will be paid as follows:

4.   The Seller acknowledges receiving the Earnest money deposit of $ _____ from the Buyer. If this sale is not completed for any valid reason, this money will be returned to the Buyer without penalty or interest.

5.   This agreement will close on _____, 19 ___, at _____ o'clock _____ . m., at _____, City of _____, State of _____. At that time, and upon payment by the Buyer of the portion of the purchase price then due, the Seller will deliver to Buyer the following documents:

   (a) ____ A Bill of Sale for all personal property

   (b) ____ A Warranty Deed for the real estate.

6.   At closing, pro-rated adjustments to the purchase price will be made for the following items:

   (a) Utilities,

   (b) Property taxes, and

   (c) The following other items:

7.   The following closing costs will be paid by the Seller:

8.   The following closing costs will be paid by the Buyer:

9.   Seller represents that it has good and marketable title to the property, and will supply the Buyer with either an abstract of title or a standard policy of title insurance. Seller further represents that the property is free and clear of any restrictions on transfer, claims, indebtedness, or liabilities except the following:

Seller also warrants that all personal property included in this sale will be delivered in working order on the date of closing.

10.   The parties also agree to the following additional terms:

11.   No modification of this Contract will be effective unless it is in writing and is signed by both the Buyer and Seller. This Contract binds and benefits both the Buyer and Seller and any successors. Time is of the essence of this contract. This document, including any attachments, is the entire contract between the Buyer and Seller. This Contract is governed by the laws of the State of _____.

_____
(Signature of seller)

_____
(Printed name of seller)

_____
(Signature of buyer)

_____
(Printed name of buyer)

OPTION TO BUY REAL ESTATE AGREEMENT

This Agreement is made on _____, 19 ___, between _____

_____, Seller, residing at _____, City of _____,

State of _____, and _____, Buyer, residing at _____,

City of _____, State of _____.

The Seller now owns the following described real estate, located at _____

_____, City of _____, State of _____:

For valuable consideration, the Seller agrees to give the Buyer an exclusive option to buy this property for the following price and on the following terms:

1.   The Buyer will pay the Seller $ _____ for this option. This amount will be credited against the purchase price of the property if this option is exercised by the Buyer. If the option is not exercised, the Seller will retain this payment.

2.   The option period will be from the date of this Agreement until _____ _____, 19 ___, at which time it will expire unless exercised.

3.   During this period, the Buyer has the option and exclusive right to buy the Seller's property mentioned above for the purchase price of $ _____. The Buyer must notify the Seller, in writing, of the decision to exercise this option.

4.   Attached to this Option Agreement is a completed Contract for the Sale of Real Estate. If the Buyer notifies the Seller, in writing, of the decision to exercise the option within the option period, the Seller and Buyer agree to sign the Contract for the Sale of Real Estate and complete the sale on the terms contained in the Contract.

5.   No modification of this Agreement will be effective unless it is in writing and is signed by both the Buyer and Seller. This Agreement binds and benefits both the Buyer and Seller and any successors. Time is of the essence of this agreement. This document, including any attachments, is the entire agreement between the Buyer and Seller. This Agreement is governed by the laws of the State of _____.

_____
(Signature of seller)

_____
(Printed name of seller)

_____
(Signature of buyer)

_____
(Printed name)

QUITCLAIM DEED

This Quitclaim Deed is made on _____, 19 ___, between _____ _____, Grantor, residing at _____, City of _____, State of _____, and _____, Grantee, residing at _____, City of _____, State of _____.

For valuable consideration, the Grantor hereby quitclaims and transfers the following described real estate to the Grantee to have and hold forever, located at _____ _____, City of _____, State of _____:

Dated _____, 19 ___.

_____
(Signature of grantor)

_____
(Printed name of grantor)

State of _____

County of _____

On _____, 19 ___, _____ personally came before me and, being duly sworn, did state that he/she is the person described in the above document and that he/she signed the above document in my presence.

_____
(Notary signature)

Notary Public, for the County of _____

State of _____

My commission expires: _____

WARRANTY DEED

This Warranty Deed is made on _____, 19 ___, between _____
_____, Grantor, residing at _____, City of _____,
State of _____, and _____, Grantee, residing at _____,
City of _____, State of _____.

For valuable consideration, the Grantor hereby sells, grants, and conveys the following described real estate, in fee simple, to the Grantee to have and hold forever, along
with all easements, rights, and buildings belonging to the above property, located at
_____, City of _____, State of ____:

Grantor warrants that it is lawful owner, has full right to convey the property, property
is free from all claims, liabilities, or indebtedness, and Grantor and its successors will
warrant and defend title to Grantee against lawful claims of all persons.

Dated _____, 19 ___.

_____
(Signature of grantor)

_____
(Printed name of grantor)

State of _____

County of _____

On _____, 19 ___, _____ personally came
before me and, being duly sworn, did state that he/she is the person described in the
above document and that he/she signed the above document in my presence.

_____
(Notary signature)

Notary Public, for the County of _____, State of _____

My commission expires: _____

AFFIDAVIT OF TITLE

This Affidavit of Title is made on _____, 19 ___, between _____ _____, Seller, residing at _____, City of _____, State of _____, for _____, Buyer, residing at _____, City of _____, State of _____.

1.   Seller certifies that it is now in possession of and is the absolute owner of the following property:

2.   Seller also states that its possession has been undisputed and that Seller knows of no fact or reason that may prevent transfer of this property to the buyer.

3.   Seller also states that no liens, contracts, debts, or lawsuits exist regarding this property, except the following:

4.   Seller finally states that it has full power to transfer full title to this property to the buyer.

_____
(Signature of seller)

_____
(Printed name of seller)

State of _____
County of _____
On _____, 19 ___, _____ personally came before me and, being duly sworn, did state that he/she is the person described in the above document and that he/she signed the above document in my presence.

_____
(Notary signature)

Notary Public, for the County of _____, State of _____
My commission expires: _____

DEED OF TRUST

This Deed of Trust is made on _____, 19 ___, between _____
_____, Grantor, residing at _____, City of _____,
State of _____, and _____, Trustee, residing at _____,
City of _____, State of _____.

1.   For valuable consideration, the Grantor hereby grants, the following described
real estate to the Trustee in TRUST, along with all easements, rights, and buildings
belonging to the above property, located at _____, City of
_____, State of _____:

2.   This Property is granted in TRUST to the Trustee to secure payment of the bal-
ance of the purchase price for the property owed to the Grantor by _____
_____ Grantee, of _____, City of _____,
State of _____.

3.   The balance of the purchase price for this property is evidenced by a Promissory
Note dated _____, 19 ___, in the principal amount of $ _____, which is
payable on or before _____, 19 ___, and bears interest at the annual
rate of _____ %, and which is payable to _____,
of _____, City of _____, State of _____.
A copy of the Promissory Note is attached and all of the terms of the note are made
part of this document.

4.   Upon evidence of full payment of the Promissory Note and satisfaction of all of the terms of the note, the Trustee shall deliver a signed Deed of Release to the Grantee.

Dated _____, 19 ___.

_____
(Signature of grantor)

_____
(Printed name of grantor)

State of _____
County of _____

On _____, 19 ___, _____ personally came before me and, being duly sworn, did state that he/she is the person described in the above document and that he/she signed the above document in my presence.

_____
(Notary signature)

Notary Public, for the County of _____
State of _____
My commission expires: _____

MORTGAGE

This Mortgage is made on _____, 19 ___, between _____ _____, Mortgagor, residing at _____, City of _____, State of _____, and _____, Mortgagee, residing at _____ _____, City of _____, State of _____.

For valuable consideration, the Mortgagor hereby mortgages, grants, and conveys the following described real estate, in fee simple, to the Mortgagee to have and hold forever, along with all easements, rights, and buildings belonging to the above property, located at _____, City of _____, State of _____:

2.   This Property is granted as security to the Mortgagee to secure payment of the balance of the purchase price for the property which is owed to the Mortgagee by the Mortgagor.

3.   The balance of the purchase price for this property is evidenced by a Promissory Note dated _____, 19 ___, in the principal amount of $ _____, which is payable on or before _____, 19 ___, and bears interest at the annual rate of _____ %, and which is payable to Mortgagee. A copy of the Promissory Note is attached and all of the terms of the note are made part of this document.

4.   Upon evidence of full payment of the Promissory Note and satisfaction of all of the terms of the note, the Mortgagee agrees to deliver a signed Release of this Mortgage to the Mortgagor.

5.   The Mortgagor warrants that she/he is lawful owner and has full right to convey the property, and that the property is free from all claims, liabilities, or indebtedness, and that the Mortgagor, and her/his successors will warrant and defend title to the Mortgagee against the lawful claims of all persons.

Dated _____, 19 ___.

_____
(Signature of mortgagor)

_____
(Printed name of mortgagor)

State of _____
County of _____

On _____, 19 ___, _____ personally came before me and, being duly sworn, did state that he/she is the person described in the above document and that he/she signed the above document in my presence.

_____
(Notary signature)
Notary Public, for the County of _____
State of _____
My commission expires: _____

CHAPTER 16

Personal Loan Documents

The documents included in this chapter are designed for use in situations in which a loan will be provided using personal property as collateral for the loan. Loans for real estate, other than a simple promissory note and mortgage or trust deed, are generally subject to more state regulations and, thus, should be handled by a real estate professional or attorney.

The legal documents for financing of loans generally employ three key documents, each of which serves a different purpose. First, there is the actual *promissory note* by which the borrower promises to repay the debt. These documents are covered in Chapter 17. Next is the *security agreement* by which the borrower puts up specific property as collateral for repayment of the loan. Finally, there is the *U.C.C. financing statement* that is used to record the lien against the personal property in the public records.

All states have adopted a version of the Uniform Commercial Code (U.C.C.). This code is a set of detailed regulations which govern the purchase and sale of goods, and financing arrangements, along with many other commercial transactions. Every state has a method of filing (on the public record) various statements relating to financing arrangements. The value of making timely filings of financing statements and other U.C.C. related matter is that the date and time of filing the statement *perfects* (or legally locks in time) the security interest that has been bargained for. The party with the earliest perfected security interest relating to a particular piece of property has priority claim to that property.

The various forms included in this chapter are as follows:

Security Agreement: This document is the document that provides the *secured party* (the party providing the loan) with the right to the collateral that the borrower has put up as security for the repayment of the loan.

The security agreement in this book provides for the following terms:

- That the borrower is granting the secured party a security interest in the property named;
- That the security interest is to secure payment of a certain obligation;
- That if the borrower defaults on the obligation, the secured party may accelerate the loan and make it immediately due and payable;
- That if the borrower defaults, the secured party will have all the remedies under the U.C.C. (these may include selling the property or keeping the property);
- That the borrower will pay any costs of collection upon default;
- That the borrower will be careful with the collateral and will not sell or dispose of it;
- That the borrower will insure the collateral and keep it at a specified address for the term of the loan period;
- That the borrower states that the property is owned free and clear, with no other liens against it, and that they have authority to use it as collateral;
- That the borrower will sign any necessary financing statements;
- That any changes to the agreement must be in writing.

Receipt for Collateral: If it is desired that the property offered as collateral be held by the secured party, it will be necessary to alter the above Security Agreement by deleting Paragraphs #5 and #6 and preparing this receipt for the collateral. This receipt provides:

- That the secured party has obtained the collateral and will hold it as security until the loan is repaid;
- That if the borrower defaults on the obligation, the property may be disposed of to satisfy the obligation;
- That the borrower will pay any costs and expenses relating to holding the property;
- That the secured party does not acknowledge the value or condition of the property offered as collateral.

Financing Statement (U.C.C.): This form is a memorandum of the details of a security arrangement. It is designed to be filed with the appropriate state filing office in order to record the security interest. Once filed, this statement serves as a public record of the date and time that the security interest in the particular property was perfected. To fill in this form, simply provide the namese and addresses of the parties and a description of the security interest being filed.

Release of Security Interest: This form acts as a release of the property from its nature as collateral for the loan. In addition, when the loan is repaid, the promissory note or obligation should also be released (See Chapter 17). To fill in this form, simply provide the names and addresses of the parties and a description of the security interest being released.

Release of U.C.C. Financing Statement: This form is a memorandum detailing the release of the financing obligation and should be filed with the state filing office to clear the records once the obligation has been satisfied. To fill in this form, simply provide the names and addresses of the parties and a description of the financing statement being released.

SECURITY AGREEMENT

This Agreement is made on _____, 19 ___, between _____ _____, Borrower, residing at _____, City of _____, State of _____, and _____, Secured Party, residing at _____, City of_____, State of _____.

For valuable consideration, the parties agree as follows:

1.   The Borrower grants the Secured Party a security interest under Article 9 of the Uniform Commercial Code in the following personal property which will be considered Collateral:

2.   This security interest is granted to secure payment by the Borrower to the Secured Party on the following obligation:

3.   In the event of default by the Borrower in payment of any of the amounts due on the obligation listed under Paragraph #2, the Secured Party may declare the entire obligation immediately due and payable and will have all of the remedies of a secured party under the Uniform Commercial Code.

4.   In the event of such default, Borrower will also be responsible for any costs of collection, including court costs and attorney fees.

5.   The Borrower agrees to use reasonable care in using the Collateral and agrees not to sell or dispose of the Collateral.

6.   The Borrower agrees to keep the Collateral adequately insured and at the following address for the entire term of this Security Agreement:

7.   The Borrower represents that the Collateral is owned free and clear and that there are no other security agreements, indebtedness, or liens relating to the property offered as Collateral. Borrower also states that it has full authority to grant this security interest.

8.   Borrower agrees to sign any financing statements that are required by the Secured Party to perfect this security interest.

9.   No modification of this Agreement will be effective unless it is in writing and is signed by both parties. This Agreement binds and benefits both parties and any successors.

10.   Time is of the essence of this agreement. This document, including any attachments, is the entire agreement between the parties. This Agreement is governed by the laws of the State of _____.

The parties have signed this Agreement on the date specified at the beginning of this Agreement.

_____
(Signature of borrower

_____
(Signature of secured party)

_____
(Printed name of borrower)

_____
(Printed name of secured party)

RECEIPT FOR COLLATERAL

This receipt is made in connection with the Promissory Note dated _____,
19___, and the Security Agreement dated _____, 19 ___, between the
Borrower _____, residing at _____,
City of _____, State of _____, and the Noteholder/ Secured Party
_____, residing at _____,
City of _____, State of _____.

The Noteholder/Secured Party acknowledges delivery of the following described personal property as collateral under the Security Agreement:

This collateral is subject to the lien and all of the conditions of the Security Agreement. In the event of the Borrower's default on any of the terms of the Note or Security Agreement, this property may be disposed of by the Noteholder/Secured Party to satisfy any of the Borrower's obligations as allowed by law.

The Borrower will continue to pay all costs and expenses relating to this property, including any maintenance, storage fees, insurance, or taxes.

This receipt does not acknowledge the condition or the value of the property retained as collateral.

Dated:_____

_____
(Signature of borrower)

_____
(Signature of secured party/noteholder)

_____
(Printed name of borrower)

_____
(Name of secured party/noteholder)

FINANCING STATEMENT (U.C.C.)

This Original Financing Statement is presented for filing under the Uniform Commercial Code as adopted in the following state: _____.

(This Section for Use of the Filing Officer)

Date of filing:_____ Time of filing: _____

Number and address of filing office:_____

_____

_____

Name(s) of Borrower: _____

Address(es) of Borrower: _____

Name(s) of Secured Party: _____

Address(es) of Secured Party: _____

This Financing Statement covers the following personal property:

This Financing Statement secures a debt document described as:

Name of document:_____ Date of document: _____

Face Value of document: $ _____ Maturity date: _____

Related terms and conditions of the debt are contained in this debt document and any other documents mentioned in the debt document.

Dated: _____

_____   SEAL
(Signature of borrower)

_____
(Printed name of borrower)

RELEASE OF SECURITY INTEREST

For valuable consideration, _____, residing at _____,
City of _____, State of _____, releases _____
residing at _____, City of _____, State of
_____, from the following specific Security Agreement, dated _____,
19 ___ :

Any claims or obligations that are not specifically mentioned are not released by this Release of Security Interest.

The Secured Party has not assigned any claims or obligations covered by this release to any other party.

The Secured Party will sign a Release of U.C.C. Financing Statement if requested by Borrower.

The party signing this release intends that it both bind and benefit any successors.

Dated:_____

_____
(Signature of secured party)

_____
(Printed name of secured party)

RELEASE OF U.C.C. FINANCING STATEMENT

This Release of Financing Statement is presented for filing under the Uniform Commercial Code as adopted in the following state: _____.

(This Section for Use of the Filing Officer)
Date of filing: _____ Time of filing: _____
Number and address of filing office: _____
_____

Name(s) of Borrower: _____
Address(es) of Borrower: _____
Name(s) of Secured Party: _____
Address(es) of Secured Party: _____
The Original Financing Statement covers the following personal property:

File # of Original Financing Statement: _____ Dated: _____
Office where Original Financing Statement was filed: _____

Dated: _____

_____   SEAL
(Signature of secured party)

_____
(Printed name of secured party)

State of _____
County of _____

On _____, 19 ___, _____ personally came before me and, being duly sworn, did state that he/she is the person described in the above document and that he/she signed the above document in my presence.

_____
(Notary signature)
Notary Public, for the County of _____
State of _____
My commission expires: _____

CHAPTER 17

PROMISSORY NOTES

Contained in this chapter are various promissory notes. A *promissory note* is a document by which a borrower promises to pay the holder of the note a certain amount of money under specific terms. In the forms in this chapter, the person who borrows the money is referred to a the *borrower* and the person to whom the borrower is to pay is referred to as the *noteholder*. The noteholder is generally the lender also, but this need not be so. The forms in this chapter are intended only for use by individuals who are not regularly in the business of lending money. Complex state and federal regulations apply to lending institutions and such rules are beyond the scope of this book. This chapter also contains various forms for demanding payments on a promissory note.

Promissory Note (Installment Repayment): This type of promissory note is a standard unsecured note. Being *unsecured* means that the noteholder has no collateral or specific property against which to foreclose should the borrower default on the note. If the borrower doesn't pay, the noteholder must sue and get a general judgement against the borrower. Collection of the judgement may then be made against the borrower's assets.

This particular note calls for the borrower to pay a certain annual interest rate on the note and to make periodic payments to the noteholder. It also has certain general terms:

- That the borrower may prepay any amount on the note without penalty;
- That if the borrower is in default, the noteholder may demand full payment on the note;
- That the note is not assumable by anyone other than the borrower;

- That the borrower waives certain formalities relating to demands for payment;
- That the borrower agrees to pay any of the costs of collection after a default.

In order to complete this form, the following information is necessary:

- The names and addresses of the borrower and the noteholder;
- The amount of the principal of the loan;
- The annual interest rate to be charged;
- The period for the installments (for example: monthly, weekly);
- The day of the period on which payments will be due;
- The number of days a payment may be late before it is considered a default.

Promissory Note (Lump Sum Repayment): This note is also an unsecured promise to pay. However, this version of a promissory note calls for the payment, including accrued interest, to be paid in one lump sum at a certain date in the future. This note has the same general conditions relating to prepayment, defaults, and assumability as the Promissory Note with Installment Payments discussed above.

To prepare this form, use the following information:

- The names and addresses of the borrower and the noteholder;
- The amount of the principal of the loan;
- The annual interest rate to be charged;
- The final due date of the lump sum payment;
- The number of days past the due date that payment may be made before the note is in default.

Promissory Note (On Demand): This also is an unsecured note. This type of promissory note, however, is immediately payable in full at any time upon the demand of the noteholder. This note has the same general conditions relating to prepayment, defaults, and assumability as the Promissory Note with Installment Payments discussed above.

The following information is necessary to complete this form:

- The names and addresses of the borrower and the noteholder;
- The amount of the principal of the loan;
- The annual interest rate to be charged;
- The number of days past the demand date that payment may be made before the note is in default.

Promissory Note (Secured): This type of promissory note is referred to as a *secured* note. What this means is that the borrower has given the noteholder some form of property or right to property as collateral for the loan. This allows the noteholder a direct claim against the specific property and the ability to foreclose against the property if the note is in default. A secured note also places the noteholder higher on the list for repayment if the borrower files for bankruptcy.

This particular form is designed to be used in conjunction with a completed Security Agreement (Chapter 16) covering the security arrangement between the borrower and the noteholder (lender). The security for this type of note must be personal property. A secured promissory note may be drawn up for use with real estate as collateral. However, since this will entail the use of a mortgage or deed of trust as the security agreement, the services of a lawyer, or real estate professional may be required. This secured promissory note is set up for installment payments. However, the language from a "demand" or "lump-sum" payment-type note can be substituted, if desired.

The conditions of this promissory note are as follows:

- That default on any of the conditions of the underlying security agreement may allow the noteholder to demand immediate full payment on the note;
- That the borrower may prepay any amount on the note without penalty;
- That if the borrower is in default, the noteholder may demand full payment on the note;
- That the note is not assumable by anyone other than the borrower;
- That the borrower waives certain formalities relating to demands for payment;
- That the borrower agrees to pay any of the costs of collection after a default.

The following information is needed to complete this form:

- The names and addresses of the borrower and the noteholder;
- The amount of the principal of the loan;
- The annual interest rate to be charged;
- The period for the installments (for example: monthly, weekly);
- The day of the period on which payments will be due;
- The date of the security agreement which coincides with the note;
- The number of days a payment may be late before it is considered a default.

Release of Promissory Note: This release is intended to be used to release a party from obligations under a Promissory Note. There are several other methods by which to accomplish this same objective. The return of the original note to the maker, clearly marked *Paid In Full* will serve the same purpose. A Receipt in Full will also accomplish this goal (see Chapter 10). The Release of Promissory Note may, however, be used in those situations when the release is based on something other than payment in full of the underlying note. For example, the note may be satisfied by a gift from the bearer of the note of release from the obligation. Another situation may involve a release of the note based on a concurrent release of a claim which the maker of the note holds against the holder of the note.

Notice of Default on Installment Promissory Note: This form will be used to notify the maker of a promissory note of their default on an installment payment on a promissory note. Notice of default should be sent promptly to any account which falls behind in their payments on a note. It provides a legal basis for a suit for breach of the promissory note.

Demand for Full Payment on Installment Promissory Note: A demand for full payment on a promissory note can only be made if the precise terms of the note allow for this. A note may have specific terms which allow it to be accelerated upon default on any payments. This means that if the maker of the note falls behind on their payments, the holder may *accelerate* all of the payment dates to the present and demand that the note be paid in full. Generally, this form will be used after giving the debtor a reasonable time to make up the missed installment payment.

Demand for Payment on Demand Promissory Note: This document should be used when you hold a promissory note which is payable on demand and you wish to demand full payment. Realistically, you should generally allow the maker of such a note a reasonable time to gather enough funds to make the payment. This form allows a period of 10 days. However, you may wish to modify this period after consulting with the debtor.

PROMISSORY NOTE
(INSTALLMENT REPAYMENT)

$ _____

Dated:_____

For value received, the Borrower _____,

residing at _____, City of _____, State of _____,

promises to pay to the Noteholder _____,

residing at _____, City of _____, State of _____,

the principal amount of $ _____, with interest at the annual rate of

_____% on any unpaid balance.

Payments are payable to the Noteholder in _____ consecutive _____ installments

of $ _____, including interest, and continuing on the _____ day of each

_____ until paid in full. If not paid off sooner, this Note is due and payable in

full on _____, 19 _____.

This Note may be prepaid in whole or in part at any time without penalty. If the Borrower is in default more than _____ days with any payment, this Note is payable upon demand of any Noteholder. This note is not assumable without the written consent of the Noteholder. The Borrower waives demand, presentment for payment, protest, and notice. In the event of any default, Borrower will be responsible for any costs of collection on this Note, including court costs and attorney fees.

_____
(Signature of borrower)

_____
(Printed name of borrower)

PROMISSORY NOTE
(LUMP SUM REPAYMENT)

$ _____

Dated:_____

For value received, the Borrower _____,

residing at _____, City of _____, State of _____,

promises to pay to the Noteholder _____,

residing at _____, City of _____, State of _____,

the principal amount of $ _____, with interest at the annual rate of

_____% on any unpaid balance.

Payment on this Note is due and payable to the Noteholder in full on or before

_____, 19 ___.

This Note may be prepaid in whole or in part at any time without penalty. If the Borrower is in default more than _____ days with payment, this Note is payable upon demand of any Noteholder. This note is not assumable without the written consent of the Noteholder. The Borrower waives demand, presentment for payment, protest, and notice. In the event of any default, Borrower will be responsible for any costs of collection on this Note, including court costs and attorney fees.

_____
(Signature of borrower)

_____
(Printed name of borrower)

PROMISSORY NOTE
(ON DEMAND)

$ _____

Dated:_____

For value received, the Borrower _____,
residing at _____, City of _____, State of _____,
promises to pay ON DEMAND to the Noteholder _____,
residing at _____, City of _____, State of _____,
the principal amount of $ _____, with interest at the rate of _____%
on any unpaid balance.

This Note may be prepaid in whole or in part at any time without penalty. This note is not assumable without the written consent of the Noteholder. The Borrower waives demand, presentment for payment, protest, and notice. In the event of such default of over _____ days in making payment, Borrower will also be responsible for any costs of collection on this Note, including court costs and attorney fees.

_____
(Signature of borrower)

_____
(Printed name of borrower)

PROMISSORY NOTE
(SECURED)

$ _____

Dated:_____

For value received, the Borrower _____,

residing at _____, City of _____, State of _____,

promises to pay to the Noteholder _____,

residing at _____, City of _____, State of _____,

the principal amount of $ _____, with interest at the rate of _____%

on any unpaid balance. Payments are payable to the Noteholder in _____ consecutive

_____ installments of $ _____, including interest, and continuing

on the _____ day of each _____ until paid in full. If not paid off sooner, this Note

is due and payable in full on _____, 19 ___.

This Note is secured by a Security Agreement dated _____, 19 ___,

which has also been signed by the Borrower. This Note may be accelerated and demand for immediate full payment made by the Noteholder upon breach of any conditions of the Security Agreement. This Note may be prepaid in whole or in part at any
time without penalty. If the Borrower is in default more than ____ days with any payment, this Note is payable upon demand of any Noteholder. This note is not assumable
without the written consent of the Noteholder. The Borrower waives demand, presentment for payment, protest, and notice. In the event of any default, Borrower will
be responsible for any costs of collection on this Note, including court costs and attorney fees.

_____
(Signature of borrower)

_____
(Printed name of borrower)

RELEASE OF PROMISSORY NOTE

In consideration of full payment of the promissory note dated _____,
19 ___, in the face amount of $ _____, the Noteholder _____,
_____ residing at _____, City of _____, State of _____,
releases and discharges the Borrower(s) _____,
residing at _____, City of _____, State of _____,
from any claims or obligations on account of this note.

The party signing this release intends that it bind and benefit both itself and any successors.

Dated: _____

_____
(Signature of noteholder)

_____
(Printed name of noteholder)

NOTICE OF DEFAULT ON INSTALLMENT PROMISSORY NOTE

Date: _____

To:

RE: Default on Promissory Note Payment

Dear _____:

Regarding the Promissory Note dated _____, 19 ___, in the original amount of $ _____, of which you are the maker, you have defaulted on the installment payment due on _____, 19___ , in the amount of $ _____.

Demand is made upon you for payment of this past-due installment payment. If payment is not received by us within 10 (ten) days from the date of this notice, we will proceed to enforce our rights under the Promissory Note for collection of the entire balance.

Very truly,

_____
(Signature)

DEMAND FOR FULL PAYMENT ON INSTALLMENT PROMISSORY NOTE

Date: _____

To:

RE: Demand for Payment on Note

Dear _____:

I am currently the holder of your Promissory Note dated _____, 19 ___, in the amount of $ _____ which is payable to _____ _____.

You have been given previous notice on _____, 19 ___, of your default on payments of this Note. Under the terms of the Note and by this notice, I am making a formal demand for payment by you of the full unpaid balance of this Note, together with all accrued interest within 10 (ten) days of receipt of this letter. Please contact me at the following address and phone number in order to initiate the payment process. If full payment is not received within 10 (ten) days from the date of this Demand, the Note shall be forwarded to our attorneys for legal collection proceedings and you will be immediately liable for all costs of collection, including additional legal and court costs. Thank you very much for your prompt attention to this serious matter.

Very truly,

_____
(Signature)

DEMAND FOR PAYMENT ON
DEMAND PROMISSORY NOTE

Date: _____

To:

RE: Demand for Payment on Note

Dear _____:

I am currently the holder of your Promissory Note dated _____, 19 __,
in the amount of $ _____ which is payable to _____
or to the holder on demand.

By this notice, I am making a formal demand for payment by you of the full unpaid
balance of this Note, together with all accrued interest, within 10 (ten) days of receipt
of this letter. The total amount due at this time is $ _____.

Please contact me at the following address and phone number in order to initiate the
payment process. If full payment is not received within 10 (ten) days from the date of
this Demand, the Note shall be forwarded to our attorneys for legal collection proceedings and you will be immediately liable for all costs of collection, including any
additional legal and court costs. Thank you very much for your prompt attention to
this serious matter.

Very truly,

_____
(Signature)

CHAPTER 18

COLLECTION DOCUMENTS

The documents contained in this chapter are for use in the collection of past-due payments which are owed to you. Through the proper use of the documents in this chapter, you should be able to collect on the majority of over-due and unpaid accounts without having to resort to the use of attorneys or collection agencies. Of course, if the initial attempts at collection using these documents fail, then it is advisable to turn the accounts over to parties who will be able to bring legal procedures to bear on the defaulting parties. The following forms are included in this chapter:

Request for Payment: This form should be used to make the initial request for payment from an overdue payment. It should be sent when you have decided that a payment due is in delinquent status. It is intended to promote payment on the overdue account. To prepare it, you will need to enter the name of the company or person with the delinquent payment; the date, amount, and of the past-due payment; any interest or late charges which have been assessed; and any credits or payments which have been made on the account. Be sure to keep a record of this request. Generally, making a copy of the actual request that is sent and placing in the file for the over-due account is the easiest method for this.

Second Request for Payment: You will generally use this form about 30 days after you have sent the first request for payment. The information necessary for this form will be the same as the first request. You will need to, however, update any additions or subtractions to the account which have taken place during the period since the first request (for example: any payments on account, additional interest charges, additional late payments, etc.).

Final Demand for Payment: This form should normally be used after 30 more days have elapsed since the second payment request was sent. It is a notice that collection proceedings will be begun if payment has not been received on the delinquent account within 10 days. (Please note that you may extend this period if you desire, for example, to allow for 30 days to pay). This notice should not be sent unless you actually plan on following up with the collection. However, it is often reasonable to wait a short while after the deadline before proceeding with assignment of the account for collection. This allows for delays in mail delivery and takes into account the tendency of companies and people with debt problems to push the time limits to the maximum. Should this demand letter fail to produce any results, you are advised to seek the assistance of a competent attorney or a reputable collection agency.

REQUEST FOR PAYMENT

Date: _____

To:

RE: Payment of Account

Dear _____ :

Regarding your loan, please be advised that we show the following outstanding balance on our books:

      TOTAL BALANCE DUE   AMOUNT $ _____

Please be advised that we have not yet received payment on this outstanding balance. We are certain that this is merely an oversight and would ask that you please send the payment now. Please disregard this notice if full payment has been forwarded to us.

Thank you for your immediate attention to this matter.

    Very truly,

_____
     (Signature)

SECOND REQUEST FOR PAYMENT

Date: _____

To:

RE: Payment of Account

Dear _____:

Regarding your loan, please be advised that we continue to show the following outstanding balance on our books:

TOTAL BALANCE DUE   AMOUNT $ _____

Please be advised that since our last request for payment dated _____, 19 ___ we have still not yet received payment on this outstanding balance. We must request that you please send the payment immediately. Please disregard this notice if full payment has been forwarded to us.

Thank you for your immediate attention to this matter.

Very truly,

_____
(Signature)

FINAL DEMAND FOR PAYMENT

Date: _____

To:

RE: Payment of Account

Dear _____:

Regarding your delinquent loan in the amount of $ _____, we have requested payment on this account several times without success.

THIS IS YOUR FINAL NOTICE.

Please be advised that unless we receive payment in full on this loan within 10 days of the date of this letter, we will immediately turn this account over to our attorneys for collection proceedings against you without further notice.

These proceedings will include claims for pre-judgement interest on your account and all legal and court-related costs in connection with collection of this past-due account and will substantially increase the amount which you owe us. Collection proceedings may also have an adverse effect on your credit rating.

We regret the necessity for this action and urge you to clear up this account delinquency immediately. If full payment has been sent, please disregard this notice. Thank you for your immediate attention to this serious matter.

Very truly,

_____
(Signature)

CHAPTER 19

MISCELLANEOUS LEGAL FORMS

Included in this chapter are various documents that may be used in a variety of circumstances. These documents range from a form for making sworn statements to an indemnity agreement that may be used by a party to accept responsibility for any claims or liability that may arise in a transaction. The forms that are included and the information necessary to prepare them are as follows:

Affidavit: This document is a basic form for an affidavit. An *affidavit* is a legal document with which a person can make a sworn statement regarding anything. It is essentially testimony, under oath, by the person making the affidavit. An affidavit may be used to document an aspect of a business transaction. It may be used for verification purposes. It may also be used as a supplement to a lawsuit, as the form provided is made under penalty of perjury.

The information necessary to prepare the basic affidavit is the name and address of the person making the affidavit and a written recital of the statement that the person is affirming. This form should be notarized as the statement is being made under oath and under penalty of perjury.

Indemnity Agreement: This form may be used as a general supplement to other transactions. With this form, one party to a transaction agrees to *indemnify* and hold the other party harmless. What this means is that the party doing the indemnifying (the *indemnifier*) will pay for and defend against any legal claims or liabilities against the person being indemnified (the *indemnitee*) that may arise in the future based on the transaction. Unfortunately, there are no other English words that carry the precise meaning necessary to name the parties in this context.

The indemnifier, by this agreement, agrees to defend against any claims or liabilities arising from the transaction. The indemnitee agrees to promptly notify the indemnifier of any such claims. If the indemnifier does not pay for or defend against such claims, the indemnitee has the right to do so and demand reimbursement from the indemnifier.

The information necessary to prepare this form is the names and addresses of the parties involved; a complete description of the transaction being indemnified; and the name of the state whose laws will govern the agreement.

General Employment Contract: This form may be used for any situation in which an employee is hired for a specific job. The issues addressed by this contract are as follows:

- That the employee will perform a certain job and any incidental further duties:
- That the employee will be hired for a certain period and for a certain salary;
- That the employee will be given certain job benefits (for example: sick pay, vacations, etc.);
- That the employee agrees to abide by the employer's rules and regulations;
- That the employee agrees to sign agreements regarding confidentiality and inventions;
- That the employee agrees to submit any employment disputes to mediation and arbitration.

The information necessary to complete this form is as follows:

- The names and addresses of the employer and employee;
- A complete description of the job:
- The date the job is to begin and the length of time that the job will last:
- The amount of compensation and benefits for the employee (salary, sick pay, vacation, retirement, and insurance benefits);
- The state whose laws will govern the contract.

Independent Contractor Agreement: An *independent contractor* may also be hired to perform a job. As opposed to an *employee*, this type of worker is defined as one who maintains their own independent business, uses their own tools, and does not work under the direct supervision of the person who has hired them. This form should be used when hiring an independent contractor. It provides a standard form for the hiring out of specific work to be performed within a set time period for a particular payment. It also provides a method for authorizing extra work under the contract. Finally, this document provides that the contractor agrees to indemnify the owner against any claims or liabilities arising from the performance of the work.

To complete this form, fill in a detailed description of the work; dates by which portions of the job are to be completed; the pay for the job; the terms and dates of payment; and the state whose laws will govern the contract.

Request for Credit Information: This form is designed to be used to obtain information regarding your personal credit history from any credit reporting agency. It is in accordance with the Federal Fair Credit Reporting Act. Fill in the appropriate information and forward it to the credit reporting agency from which you wish to obtain information.

Notice of Disputed Account: This form should be used by you if you have received a statement with which you disagree. If you feel that the statement is in error, spell out your reasoning in the space provided and send this form to the creditor.

Notice of Dishonored Check: This document should be sent to anyone whose bad check has been returned to you from a bank. It is generally a good idea to attempt to have the check cleared twice before beginning the collection process with this letter. This provides time for last minute deposits to clear and will often allow the check to clear. This document gives notice to the person of the dishonored check, notifies them of your policy and charges regarding service charges for bad checks, and provides a time limit for clearing up the bad check prior to legal action. Once the check has been paid, return the original check to the debtor.

Stop Payment on Check Order: This form is intended to be provided to a bank or similar financial institution to confirm a telephone stop payment request. This form provides the institution with written confirmation of the oral request to stop payment on a check.

AFFIDAVIT

State of _____

County of _____

I, _____, being of legal age, make the following statements and declare that, on my own personal knowledge, they are true:

Signed under the penalty of perjury on _____ , 19 __.

_____
(Signature)

_____
(Printed name)

On _____, 19 __, _____ personally came before me and, being duly sworn, did state that he/she is the person described in the above document and that he/she signed the above document in my presence.

_____
(Notary signature)
Notary Public, for the County of _____
State of _____
My commission expires: _____

INDEMNITY AGREEMENT

This Indemnity Agreement is made on _____, 19 ___, between _____ _____, the Indemnifier, residing at _____, City of _____, State of ____, and _____, the Indemnitee, residing at _____, City of_____, State of ____.

For valuable consideration, the parties agree as follows:

1.   The Indemnifier agrees to indemnify and save the Indemnitee harmless from any claim or liability arising from the following activity:

2.   In the event of any claim or asserted liability against the Indemnitee arising from the above activity, the Indemnitee agrees to provide the Indemnifier with prompt written notice. Upon notice, the Indemnifier agrees to defend and save the Indemnitee harmless from any loss or liability. In the event the Indemnifier fails to indemnify the Indemnitee, the Indemnitee has the right to defend or settle any claim on their own behalf and be full reimbursed by the Indemnifier for all costs and expenses of such defense or settlement.

3.   No modification of this Agreement will be effective unless it is in writing and is signed by both parties. This Agreement binds and benefits both parties and any successors. This document, including any attachments, is the entire agreement between the parties. This Agreement is governed by the laws of the State of _____.

Dated:_____

_____
(Signature of indemnifier)

_____
(Signature of indemnitee)

_____
(Printed name of indemnifier)

_____
(Printed name of indemnitee)

GENERAL EMPLOYMENT CONTRACT

This Contract is made on _____, 19 ___, between _____ _____, Employer, residing at _____, City of _____, State of _____, and _____, Employee, residing at _____ _____, City of _____, State of _____.

For valuable consideration, the Employer and Employee agree as follows:

1.   The Employee agrees to perform the following duties and job description:

The Employee also agrees to perform further duties incidental to the general job description. This is considered a full time position.

2.   The Employee will begin work on _____, 19 ___. This position shall continue for a period of _____ .

3.   The Employee will be paid the following:
    Weekly salary:
The Employee will also be given the following benefits:
    Sick Pay:
    Vacations:
    Bonuses:
    Retirement Benefits:
    Insurance Benefits:

4.   The Employee agrees to abide by all rules and regulations of the Employer at all times while employed.

5.   This Contract may be terminated by:
    (a)   Breach of this Contract by the Employee;
    (b)   The expiration of this Contract without renewal;
    (c)   Death of the employee;

(d)   Incapacitation of the Employee for over _____days in any one year.

6.   The Employee agrees to sign the following additional documents as a condition to obtaining employment:

(a)   Employee Confidentiality Agreement

(b)   Employee Patents and Invention Agreement

7.   Any dispute between the Employer and Employee related to this Contract will be settled by voluntary mediation. If mediation is unsuccessful, the dispute will be settled by binding arbitration using an arbitrator of the American Arbitration Association.

8.   Any additional terms of this Contract:

9.   No modification of this Contract will be effective unless it is in writing and is signed by both the Employer and Employee. This Contract binds and benefits both parties and any successors. Time is of the essence of this Contract. This document is the entire agreement between the parties. This Contract is governed by the laws of the State of _____.

Dated:_____

_____
(Signature of employer)

_____
(Printed name of employer)

_____
(Signature of employee)

_____
(Printed name of employee)

INDEPENDENT CONTRACTOR AGREEMENT

This Agreement is made on _____, 19 ___, between _____
_____, Owner, residing at _____, City of _____,
State of _____, and _____, Contractor, residing at _____,
City of _____, State of _____.

For valuable consideration, the Owner and Contractor agree as follows:

1.   The Contractor agrees to furnish all of the labor and materials to do the following work for the Owner as an independent contractor:

2.   The Contractor agrees that the following portions of the total work will be completed by the dates specified:

<u>Work</u>   <u>Date</u>

3.   The Contractor agrees to perform this work in a workmanlike manner according to standard practices. If any plans or specifications are part of this job, they are attached to and are part of this Contract.

4.   The Owner agrees to pay the Contractor as full payment $ _____ ,
for doing the work outlined above. This price will be paid to the Contractor on satisfactory completion of the work in the following manner and on the following dates:

5.   The Contractor and Owner may agree to extra services and work, but any such extras must be set out and agreed to in writing by both the Contractor and the Owner.

6.   The Contractor agrees to indemnify and hold the Owner harmless from any claims or liability arising from the Contractor's work under this Contract.

7.   No modification of this Contract will be effective unless it is in writing and is signed by both parties. This Contract binds and benefits both parties and any successors. Time is of the essence of this contract. This document, including any attachments, is the entire agreement between the parties. This Contract is governed by the laws of the State of _____.

       Dated:_____

_____
       (Signature of owner)

_____
       (Printed name of owner)

_____
       (Signature of contractor)

_____
       (Printed name of contractor)

REQUEST FOR CREDIT INFORMATION

To:

RE: Disclosure of Credit Information

By this letter, I hereby request complete disclosure of my personal credit file as held within your agency records. This request is in accordance with the Federal Fair Credit Reporting Act. I request that this disclosure provide the names and addresses of any parties who have received a copy of my credit report, and the names and addresses of any parties who have provided information that is contained in my credit report.

Name: _____

Prior or other Name: _____

Address:_____

Prior or other address: _____

Social Security # _____ Phone # _____

Dated: _____

_____
(Signature)

State of _____

County of _____

On _____, 19 __, _____ personally came before me and, being duly sworn, did state that he/she is the person described in the above document and that he/she signed the above document in my presence.

_____
(Notary Signature)

Notary Public, for the County of ____, State of _____

My commission expires:

NOTICE OF DISPUTED ACCOUNT

Date: _____

To:

RE: Account Payable

Dear _____:

We are in receipt of your statement of our account dated _____, 19____, indicating a balance due you of $ _____.

We dispute this amount due for the following reasons:

Please contact us immediately to discuss the adjustment of our account.

    Very truly,

_____
    (Signature)

NOTICE OF DISHONORED CHECK

Date: _____

To:

Dear _____:

Please be advised that payment on your Check #_____, dated _____,
19 ___, in the amount of $ _____, has been refused by your bank
_____, of _____, City of _____,
State of _____. We have verified with your bank that there are insufficient
funds to pay the check.

Therefore, we request that you immediately replace this check with cash or a certified
check for the amount of the bad check and an additional $ _____
as our service charge.

Unless we receive such payment within 10 (ten) days from the date of this letter, or
such further time as may be allowed by state law, we will immediately commence appropriate legal action for recovery of our funds. Please be advised that such legal proceedings may substantially increase the amount owed to us and may include pre-
judgement interest and legal and court costs.

Upon receipt of payment, we will return your check to you. Thank you for your
prompt response to this serious matter.

_____
(Signature)

STOP PAYMENT ON CHECK ORDER

Date: _____

To:

RE: Stop Payment on Check

Dear:

Pursuant to our telephone conversation of _____, 19 ___, please stop payment on the following check:

Account Name:
Account #:
Check #:
Check Date:
Check Amount:
Payable to:

Thank you for your immediate attention to this matter.

    Very truly,

_____
    (Signature)

GLOSSARY

Acknowledgement: Formal declaration before a Notary Public.

Action: A lawsuit or proceeding in a court of law.

Administrator/Administratrix: One who is appointed to administer the estate of a deceased person who has died without a will or who has died with a will but has not named an Executor. The distinction between the two titles (male and female) has largely been removed and Administrator is proper usage for either male or female.

Affidavit: A written statement of facts which is made under oath and which is signed before a notary public or court official.

Agent: A person who is authorized to act on behalf of another. A corporation acts only through its agents, whether they are directors, employees, or officers.

Agreement: A verbal or written resolution of disputed issues.

Alimony: A payment of support for one spouse provided by the other spouse. May be paid in periodic payments, in one lump-sum payment, or a combination of both. May be paid temporarily or on a permanent basis. (Same as spousal support or maintenance.)

Assignment: The transfer of ownership in property, either in whole or in part.

Attestation: To sign one's name as a witness to a will.

Beneficiary: One who is named in a will to receive property; one who receives a benefit or gift, as under the terms of a trust.

Bequest: Traditionally, a gift of personal property in a will. Synonymous with legacy. Now, "gift" is the appropriate usage for either a gift of real estate or personal property.

Civil lawsuit: A lawsuit based on a private wrong, as opposed to a public wrong or criminal act.

Claim: A charge by one person against another.

Codicil: A formally signed supplement to a will.

Community property: Generally, all income and property which is acquired by either or both spouses during the course of a marriage, except property acquired by individual gift or inheritance. Community property does not include property that was acquired prior to a marriage. In most community property states, both spouses are considered to own an equal share of all of the community property. (See separate property.)

Consideration: In contract law, a mutually bargained-for exchange of something of value.

Contested divorce: A divorce where at least one issue has not been settled prior to court. A court must decide any issues that have not been agreed upon in a contested case.

Contract: An agreement between two or more parties which is enforceable by law.

Costs: The expenses of bringing or defending a lawsuit. A court award of "costs" in a case to either party does not, generally, include payment for attorney's fees.

Counter-claim: A complaint (or petition) filed by a defendant (or respondent) which states claims against the plaintiff (or petitioner.)

Damages: Monetary compensation asked for in a law suit by a person or entity which has suffered a loss or injury due to a unlawful, reckless, or negligent act of another.

Decedent: One who has died.

Defendant: The person who defends against a lawsuit brought against him or her by another. (See respondent.)

Dissolution of marriage: A legal judgement that severs the marriage of two people and restores them to the status of single persons. (Same as divorce.)

Divorce: A legal judgement that severs the marriage of two people and restores them to the status of single persons. (Same as dissolution of marriage.)

Domicile: A person's principal and permanent home.

Equitable division: A method of property division in a divorce (or dissolution of marriage) which is generally based on a variety of factors in an attempt to allocate a fair and just amount of property to each spouse.

Escheat: The reversion of property to the state, if there is no family member found to inherit it.

Estate: All property owned by a person.

Execution: The formal signing of a will.

Executor/Executrix: The person appointed in a will to carry out the testator's wishes and to administer the property.

Fault-based divorce: A type of divorce which may only be granted on a showing that one of the spouses was guilty of some form of marital misconduct.

Fiduciary: A person with a duty of care to another. For example, a trustee has a duty of care to any beneficiary of a trust, and, thus, is a fiduciary.

Gift: A voluntary transfer of property to another without any compensation.

Guardian: A person with the legal power and duty to care for another person and/or a person's property.

Heirs: Those persons who inherit from a person by operation of law if there is no will present.

Hold-harmless: A phrase used to describe an agreement by which one person agrees to assume full liability for an obligation and protect another from any loss or expense based on that obligation.

Holographic: A will that is entirely handwritten by the testator and unwitnessed. No longer valid in most states.

Indemnify: To reimburse or compensate. Directors and officers of corporations are often reimbursed or indemnified for all the expenses they may have incurred in incorporating.

Intestate: To die without leaving a valid will.

Joint property: Property which is held or titled in the name of more than one person. (See joint tenancy, community property, and marital property.)

Joint tenancy: A form of joint ownership of property by which each joint owner has an equal share in the property. Generally, a joint tenancy is used in connection with a right of survivorship. (See right of survivorship.)

Jurisdiction: The power or authority of a court to rule in a particular case. A court must have jurisdiction over both the subject matter of the case and the people involved in the dispute in order to have the authority to hear a case and make binding decisions.

Legacy: A gift of personal property in a will. Now, "gift" is the appropriate usage for either a gift of real estate or personal property. Synonymous with bequest.

Legal separation: A legal lawsuit for support while the spouses are living separate and apart. A legal separation may deal with the same issues as in a divorce, but does not dissolve the marriage. (See separate maintenance.)

Lump-sum alimony: Spousal support that is made in a single payment or is a fixed amount, but paid in specific installments.

Maintenance: Support for a spouse provided by the other spouse. May be paid in periodic payments, in one lump-sum payment, or a combination of both. May be paid temporarily or on a permanent basis. Same as alimony or spousal support.

Marital property: Term used to describe the property which is subject to division by a court upon divorce or dissolution. Generally, all property which was acquired during a marriage by either or both spouses, except individual gifts and inheritances. Marital property does not generally include property that was acquired by either spouse prior to the marriage. (See community property, joint property, separate property, non-marital property.)

Marital settlement Agreement: A written agreement entered into by divorcing spouses that spells out their rights and agreements regarding property, support, and children. (Same as a separation agreement.)

Negligence: Failure to act as a reasonable person.

No-fault divorce: A type of divorce which may be granted without the necessity of showing that either spouse was guilty of some form of marital misconduct.

Non-marital property: Term used to describe separate property in some states which provide for the equitable distribution of property. Generally, non-marital property consists of property acquired prior to a marriage and property acquired by individual gift or inheritance either before or during a marriage. (See marital property, community property, and separate property.)

Nuncupative: An oral will, usually during a person's last illness and later reduced to writing by another. No longer valid in most states.

Partnership: A business owned and operated by two or more persons or organizations.

Per capita: Equally; share and share alike. For example: if a gift is made to ones' descendants, per capita, and one has two children and two grandchildren and one of the children dies, then the gift is divided equally among the surviving child and the two grand-children. This amounts to one-third to the child and one-third to each grand-child.

Per stirpes: To share by representation. For example: if a gift is made to two children, per stirpes, and one should die but leave two grand-children, the deceased child's share is given to the two grand-children in equal shares. This amounts then to one-half to the surviving child and one-fourth to each of the grand-children.

Personal property: Movable property, as opposed to real estate.

Personal representative: A person who is appointed to administer a deceased's estate. Modern usage which replaces Executor and/or Administrator.

Plaintiff: A person or entity who files a law suit in court against another.

Prenuptial agreement: A legal contract signed by two people before they get married. Such an agreement generally limits a spouse's rights to property, support, or inheritance upon divorce. (Same as a premarital agreement.)

Probate: The court proceeding to determine the validity of a will and, in general, the administration of the property which passes under the will.

Real estate/real property: Land and that which is attached permanently to it, as opposed to personal property.

Residence: The place where a person lives. (Generally, same as domicile.)

Residuary: The remainder of an estate after all debts, taxes, and gifts have been distributed.

Revocation: The annulment of a document, which renders it invalid.

Right of survivorship: The right of joint owners of a piece of property to automatically be given the other's share of the property upon the death of the other owner. This right must, generally, be specifically stated on any documents of title for it to apply. For example: a joint tenancy with the right of survivorship.

Separate maintenance: A lawsuit for support in a situation where the spouses live separate and apart but are not presently pursuing a divorce or dissolution. (Same as a legal separation.)

Separate property: Property considered to be owned individually by one spouse and not subject to division upon divorce in most states. Separate property generally consists of property acquired prior to a marriage and property acquired by individual gift or inheritance either before or during a marriage. (See marital property, community property, and non-marital property.)

Separation agreement: A written agreement entered into by divorcing spouses that spells out their rights and agreements regarding property, support, and children. (Same as a marital settlement agreement.)

Settlement agreement: The written version of a settlement which resolves certain issues. It is generally a valid contract.

Sole proprietorship: A business owned and operated by one person.

Spousal support: Support for a spouse provided by the other spouse. May be paid in periodic payments, in one lump-sum payment, or a combination of both. May be paid temporarily or on a permanent basis. (Same as alimony or maintenance.)

Spouse's share: (Same as "Statutory Share").

Statutory share: In "common law" states, that portion of a person's property that a spouse is entitled to by law, regardless of any provisions in a will. In "community property" states, a surviving spouse receives 1/2 of all of the community property, regardless of any provisions in a will.

Stipulation: An agreement, usually written, by which both sides to an issue reach an understanding on any matter.

Subpoena: A document which is served upon (delivered to) a person who is not directly involved in a lawsuit, requesting that he or she appear in court to give testimony.

Summons: A document which is served upon (delivered to) a person who is named as a defendant or respondent in a lawsuit. The summons notifies the person that the lawsuit has been filed against him or her and tells them that they have a certain time limit in which to file an answer or response in reply.

Tenancy-by-the-entireities: A form of joint ownership in which two married persons hold title to a piece of property in equal shares and each has an automatic right to the other's share upon death.

Tenancy-in-common: A form of joint ownership in which two or more persons own particular shares of a piece of property. The shares need not be equal and the persons have no legal right to any shares of another upon death.

Testamentary: The expression of intent to dispose of property by will.

Testator/Testatrix: A male or female who makes a will.

Trust: In general, property held by one party, the trustee, for the benefit of another party, the beneficiary.

Trustee: A person appointed to administer a trust.

Uncontested divorce: A divorce proceeding in which their is no dispute as to any of the legal issues involved. The lack of dispute may be because the other spouse is missing, refuses to participate in the proceeding, or agrees with the other spouse on all issues.

Waiver: A written document that relinquishes a person's rights.

Will: A formally signed and witnessed document by which a person makes a disposition of his or her property to take effect upon death.

INDEX

Nova Publishing Company's
Legal Self-Help Series

The Complete Book of Personal Legal Forms

A comprehensive reference containing over 100 easy-to-use legal documents for use by individuals and families. Contains instructions and forms for preparing contracts, wills, living wills, living trusts, pre-marital agreements, marital separation agreements, leases, bills of sale, real estate documents, and many more.

(ISBN 935755-10-1)   248 pages   **$16.95**

The Complete Book of Small Business Legal Forms

A valuable business reference book containing over 125 simplified legal documents specially prepared for use by small businesses. Contains all of the forms needed to operate any small business: forms for setting up a sole proprietorship or partnership, contracts, buying and selling goods or real estate, borrowing money, collecting overdue accounts, leases, employment contracts, promissory notes, and many more.

(ISBN 935755-03-9)   248 pages   **$17.95**

The Complete Book of Corporate Legal Forms

A thorough guide to starting and operating a small business corporation, containing over 100 legal documents designed for easy use. Everything necessary to form your own corporation: articles of incorporation, by-laws, minutes of meetings, resolutions, stock certificates, "S" corporation election, income tax forms, and much more.

(ISBN 935755-08-X)   248 pages   **$18.95**

Divorce Yourself: The National No-Fault Divorce Kit

The only guide to divorce that provides instructions and forms to allow anyone to obtain a no-fault divorce in any state without a lawyer. Contains information for dividing your property, child custody and visitation, child support, alimony, courtroom instructions. Selected as one of the "Best Law Books of the Year" by *Library Journal*.

(ISBN 935755-06-3)   315 pages   **$24.95**

Prepare Your Own Will: The National Will Kit

The most critically-acclaimed book on how to prepare your own will. Contains all of the simplified forms and instructions you will need to easily prepare your own will in the privacy of your own home. Also features instructions for living wills. A featured selection of the *Prevention Magazine Book Club*.

(ISBN 935755-07-1)   248 pages   **$15.95**

The legal forms and documents in all of Nova Publishing Company's books are valid in all 50 states and Washington D.C. These books are updated periodically to keep them current with the ever-changing laws in the U.S. All of these books are available at fine bookstores everywhere or they may be ordered with a MasterCard or Visa directly from:

National Book Network
4720 Boston Way
Lanham MD 20706

Phone: (800)462-6420
FAX: (301)459-2118